THE ARTS & CRAFTS
OF ANCIENT EGYPT

Wood-carving of Ra-hesy

THE ARTS
& CRAFTS
— OF —
ANCIENT EGYPT
FLINDERS PETRIE

SENATE

The Arts & Crafts of Ancient Egypt

First published in 1909 by T. N. Foulis Ltd,
Edinburgh and London

This edition published in 1996 by Senate,
an imprint of Tiger Books International PLC,
26A York Street, Twickenham,
Middlesex TW1 3LJ, United Kingdom

3 5 7 9 10 8 6 4 2

ISBN 1 85170 537 6

Printed and bound in the UK by
Cox & Wyman, Reading, England

PREFACE

THIS present handbook is intended to aid in the understanding of Egyptian art, and the illustrations and descriptions are selected for that purpose only. The history of the art would require a far greater range of examples, in order to illustrate the growth and decay of each of the great periods; whereas here only the most striking works of each period are shown, in order to contrast the different civilisations. The origins and connections of the art in each age are scarcely touched, and the technical details are only such as are needed to see the conditions of the art. The archaeology of the subject would need as wide a treatment as the history, and these subjects can only appear here incidentally.

It should be noticed that the divisions of artistic periods are often not the same as those of political history. Politically, the history divides at the XVIIth dynasty with the fall of the Hyksos, and at the XXIInd dynasty with the rise of the Delta

PREFACE

government. But artistically the changes are under Tahutmes I, when Syrian influences broke in, and under the XXVIth dynasty, when the classical Greeks began to dominate the art.

The effect of foreign influence in art is quite apart from political power; it is due to rival activities which may or may not mean a physical domination. The reader should ponder different cases, such as those of the spiral design of early Europe entering Egypt, of the Syrian and Cretan art in the XVIIIth dynasty, of the effect of Persia upon Greece, and of Greece upon Italy (both through Magna Graecia and the conquest of Greece), of the effect of the Goth, Lombard, and Northman on Europe, and of Japan on modern Europe. Some reflection on these great artistic movements will give a little insight as to the history of art.

Regarding the illustrations, I have thought it more useful to give details large enough to be clearly seen, rather than to contract too much surface into a space where it cannot well be studied. Portions of subjects are therefore often preferred to ral views of a whole. The outlines of artistic value, such as contours of faces or figures, are left quite untouched, as an outline cannot be taken seriously which is dependent on the block-maker

PREFACE

clearing a white or black ground. This latter treatment, unfortunately, puts out of artistic use many of the lavishly spaced plates of the Cairo Catalogue, where art is subjected to bibliophily. The liberal policy of all publications and photographs of the Cairo Museum being free of copyright, has enabled me to use many of the excellent untouched photographs of Brugsch Pasha and others. My best thanks are due to Freiherr von Bissing and the publisher of his *Denkmaeler Aegypt. Sculptur*, for permission to use figures 39, 44, 46, 48, 62, 111, and 112 from that work. Over a third of the illustrations here are from my own photographs not yet published, and principally taken for this volume.

W. M. F. P.

PERIODS AND KINGS REFERRED TO IN THIS VOLUME

Period.	Dynasty.	Names.	B.C.
Prehistoric.			8000–5500
Early kings.	I.	Narmer, Mena, Zer, . . .	5500–5400
	II.	Khasekhem, ...	5000
	III.	Zeser, Senoferu, . . .	4900–4700
Pyramid age : Old Kingdom.	IV.	Khufu, Khafra, Menkaura, .	4700–4500
	V.	Noferarkara, Unas, . .	4400–4200
	VI.	Pepy II, ...	4100–4000
	IX.	Khety, ...	3800
Middle Kingdom.	XI.	Antef V, ...	3500
	XII.	Senusert I, Senusert II, Senusert III,	3400–3300
		Amenemhat III, . . .	3300–3259
	XIII.	Hor, ...	3200
New Kingdom.	XVIII.	Aahmes, Queens Aah-hotep, Aahmes,	1587–1562
		Tahutmes I, Tahutmes II, Hatshepsut,	1541–1481
		Tahutmes III, Amenhotep II, Tahutmes IV,	1481–1414
		Amenhotep III, Akhenaten, Tutankhamen,	1414–1344
	XIX.	Sety I, Ramessu II, Merenptah, .	1326–1214
		Sety II, Tausert, . . .	1214–1203
	XX.	Ramessu III, IV, XII, . .	1202–1129
	XXI.	Isiemkheb, ...	1050
	XXII.	Shishak kings, . . .	952–749
	XXIII.	Pedubast, Pefaabast, . .	755–725
Ethiopian.	XXV.	Amenardys, Taharqa, Tanutamen,	720–664
Saite.	XXVI.	Aahmes II, ...	570–526
	XXX.	Nekhthorheb (Nectanebo), .	378–361
Ptolemies.		Cleopatra Cocce, . . .	130–106
Romans.			30–A.D. 640

CONTENTS

ix

LIST OF ILLUSTRATIONS

xi

LIST OF ILLUSTRATIONS

xii

LIST OF ILLUSTRATIONS

xiii

LIST OF ILLUSTRATIONS

LIST OF ILLUSTRATIONS

LIST OF ILLUSTRATIONS

Arts and Crafts of Ancient Egypt

CHAPTER I

THE CHARACTER OF EGYPTIAN ART

THE art of a country, like the character of the inhabitants, belongs to the nature of the land. The climate, the scenery, the contrasts of each country, all clothe the artistic impulse as diversely as they clothe the people themselves. A burly, florid Teuton in his furs and jewellery, and a lithe brown Indian in his waist-cloth, would each look entirely absurd in the other's dress. There is no question of which dress is intrinsically the best in the world; each is relatively the best for its own conditions, and each is out of place in other conditions. So it is with art: it is the expression of thought and feeling in harmony with its own conditions. The only bad art is that which is mechanical, where the impulse to give expression has decayed, and it is reduced to mere copying of styles and motives which do not belong to its actual conditions. An age of copying is the only despicable age.

It is but a confusion of thought, therefore, to try to pit the art of one country against that of another. A Corinthian temple, a Norman church, or a Chinese pavilion are each perfect in their own conditions; but if the temple is of Aberdeen granite, the church of Pacific island coral, and the pavilion amid the Brighton downs, they are each of them hopelessly wrong. To understand any art we must first begin by grasping its conditions, and feeling the contrasts, the necessities, the atmosphere, which underlie the whole terms of expression.

Now the essential conditions in Egypt are before all, an overwhelming sunshine; next, the strongest of contrasts between a vast sterility of desert and the most prolific verdure of the narrow plain; and thirdly, the illimitable level lines of the cultivation, of the desert plateau, and of the limestone strata, crossed by the vertical precipices on either hand rising hundreds of feet without a break. In such conditions the architecture of other lands would look weak or tawdry. But the style of Egypt never fails in all its varieties and changes.

The brilliancy of light led to adopting an architecture of blank walls without windows. The reflected light through open doorways was enough to show most interiors ; and for chambers far from the outer door, a square opening about six inches each way in the roof, or a slit along the wall a couple of inches high, let in sufficient light. The results of this system were, that as the walls were not divided by structural features, they were dominated by the scenes that were carved upon them. The wall surface ceased to be regarded as part of a building, and became an expansion of the papyrus or tablet. The Egyptian belief in the magical value of representations led to the figuring of the various parts of the worship on the walls of the temples or tombs, so that the divine service should be perpetually renewed in figure ; and thus what we see is not so much a building in the ordinary sense, as an illustrated service-book enclosing the centre of worship. Another result of the fierce indirect light was that which dominated sculpture. The reliefs, beautiful as they often were, would not be distinct in the diffuse facing light ; hence strong colouring was applied to render them clear and effective. So much did colouring take the lead that the finest sculptures were often smothered in a stucco facing, laid on to receive the colour. This almost spiteful ignoring of the delicate craft of the sculptor is seen in the XIIth dynasty, and was the ruling method in Ptolemaic work.

The extreme contrast between the desert and the cultivation gave its tone to the artistic sense of the people. On either hand, always in sight, there rose the margin of the boundless waste without life or verdure, the dreaded region of evil spirits and fierce beasts, the home of the nomads that were always ready to swoop on unprotected fields and cattle, if they did not sit down on the borders and eat up the country. Between these two expanses of wilderness lay the narrow strip of richest earth, black, wet, and fertile under the powerful sun; teeming with the force of life, bearing the greenest of crops, as often in the year as it could be watered. In parts may be seen three full crops of corn or beans raised each year beneath the palms that also give their annual burden of fruit; fourfold does the rich ground yield its ever-growing stream of life.

This exuberance amid absolute sterility is reflected in the proportion between the minuteness of detail and the vastness of the architecture. The

1. The barren desert background
2. The luxuriance of the plain

most gigantic buildings may have their surfaces crowded with delicate sculpture and minute colouring. What would be disproportionate elsewhere, seems in harmony amid such natural contrasts.

The strongly marked horizontal and vertical lines of the scenery condition the style of buildings that can be placed before such a background. As the temples were approached, the dominant line was the absolute level of the green plain of the Nile valley, without a rise or slope upon it. Behind the building the sky line was the level top of the desert plateau, only broken by an occasional valley, but with never a peak rising above it. And the face of the cliffs that form the stern setting is ruled across with level lines of strata, which rise in a step-like background or a wall lined across as with courses of masonry. The weathering of the cliffs breaks up the walls of rock into vertical pillars with deep shadows between them. In the face of such an overwhelming rectangular framing any architecture less massive and square than that of Egypt would be hopelessly defeated. The pediments of Greece, the circular arches of Rome, the pointed arches of England, would all seem crushed by so stern a setting. The harmony is shown most clearly in the temple of Deir el Bahri (fig. 1) below its cliffs which overshadow it. Let any other kind of building be set there, and it would be an impertinent intrusion ; the long level lines of the terraces and roofs, the vertical shadows of the colonnades, repose in perfect harmony with the mass of Nature around them. The Egyptian was quite familiar with the arch : he constantly used it in brickwork on a large scale, and he imitated its curve in stone ; yet he always hid it in his building, and kept it away from the external forms, instinctively knowing that it could not serve any part of his decorative construction.

These principles, which were thus imposed on the architecture of Egypt, were doubly enforced upon its sculpture. Not only did Nature set the framing of plain and cliff, but her work was reflected and reiterated by the massive walls, square pillars, and flat architraves, amid which Egyptian sculpture had to take its place. In such shrines it would be disastrously incongruous to place a Victory poising on one foot, or a dancing faun. They belong to the peaks of Greece, divided by rushing streams. and clothed with woods,—to a transient world of fleeting beauty, not to a landscape and an architecture of eternity. Egyptian art, however luxurious, however playful it might be, was always framed on a tacit groundwork of its natural conditions. Within those conditions there was scope for most vivid portraiture, most beautiful harmony, most delicate expression, but the Egyptian was wise enough to know his conditions and to obey them. In that obedience lay his greatness.

The truest analysis of art—that of Tolstoy—results in defining it as a means of communicating emotion. It may be the emotion produced by beauty or by loathsomeness; each expression is equally art, though each is not equally desirable art. The emotion may be imparted by words, by forms, by sounds; all are equally vehicles of different kinds of art. But without imparting an emotional perception to the mind there is no art. The emotion may be the highest, that of apprehending character, and the innate meaning of mind and of Nature; or it may be the lower form of sharing in the transient interests and excitements of others; or the basest form of all, that of enjoying their evil. How does the Egyptian appear under this analysis? What emotions can we consider were intended by his art? How far did he succeed in imparting them to the spectators?

To understand the mind of the artist we must look to those qualities which in their literature were held up as the ideals of life. Stability and Strength were the qualities most admired, and the name for public monuments was "firm things." Assuredly all mankind has looked on the works of Egypt as giving a sense of these qualities before all others. Closely connected is the sense of Endurance, which was enjoined in words, and carried into practice in the laborious work on the hardest rocks. It was for endurance that statues were made of diorite or granite, though they were painted with life-like hues, so that their material was scarcely seen. Upon these primary qualities was built a rich and varied character, reflected in the elaborate and beautiful sculpture which covered, but never interfered with, the grand mass of a monument. Truth and Justice were qualities much sought for in life, and were expressed by the artist in the reality of his immense blocks of stone, often more hidden than seen, and in the fair and even bearing of all material, without any tricks or paradoxes of structure. In all his earlier work his monolith columns and pillars were a protest that a structural unit must express unity, that what supports others must not be in itself divided. The Discipline and Harmony which were looked on as the bond of social life are shown by the subordination of the whole, by the carrying out of single schemes of decoration illustrating the use of every part of a building on all its walls, by the balance of the proportions of the whole so that there seems a perfect fitness of connection through all parts. And the happy union of vigorous Action with prudent Reserve, which showed the wise man in the proverbs, is the basis of those life-like scenes which cover the walls of the tombs, but which never betray the artist into attempting impossibilities or revealing too much.

As true art, then—that is, the expression of his being, and the communication to others of his best feelings and sense of things—the Egyptian work must stand on the highest plane of reality. It would have been a falsehood to his nature to aspire, as a Gothic architect sometimes did, in towers and pinnacles which crush their foundations and will not hold together without incongruous bonds. Nor did he wish to express the romantic sense of beauty, in structure which may tend to exceed the limits of stability. All that belongs to the atmosphere of troubadours and knights errant. The Egyptian possessed in splendid perfection the sense of Strength, Permanence, Majesty, Harmony, and effective Action, tempered with a sympathy and kindliness which cemented a vast disciplined fabric. And these aims of life as a whole he embodied and expressed in his art, with a force and truth which has impressed his character on all who look on his works. He fulfils the canon of true art as completely as any race that has come after him.

CHAPTER II

THE PERIODS AND SCHOOLS

BEFORE we can understand any art the first step is
to discriminate between the different periods and
their various styles, and to observe the characteristics of the several schools. If we consider medieval architecture, we separate the many periods from
Saxon to Renaissance; if we turn to painting, we distinguish many stages between Cimabue and Cana-
letto, yet these variations belong but to a single
revolution of civilisation, and are comprised within
some centuries; in Egyptian art we have to deal
with seven revolutions of civilisation and thousands of years. And not only the period, but also
the source and traditions of each local branch of
the art are to be recognised, and we discriminate
a dozen schools of painting between Rome and
Venice, each with its own style. So in Egypt we
need to learn the various schools and understand

their differences. In this chapter we shall notice the essential characters of each period and school as compared together; while in the following chapters the more technical detail of the statuary, reliefs, and paintings will be considered.

In order to grasp more readily the differences of period and of place, there are given here eight typical examples of different periods (figs. 3 to 10), and four examples of different schools during one reign (figs. 11 to 14). These may be supplemented by reference to subsequent illustrations, but the contrasts will be more readily seen in a simultaneous view.

The Prehistoric work (8000–5500 B.C.) shows much more mechanical than artistic ability. The treatment of the hardest materials was masterful; granite and porphyry were wrought as freely as limestone and alabaster; perfectly regular forms of vases were cut entirely by hand without any lathe. But with this there was a very tentative idea of animate forms. The feet and hands were omitted, and limbs ended only in points. The form of an outline was not thought to imply a solid, and it needed to be hatched over with cross lines (fig. 3) to show that it was a continuous body. The noses of animals are frequently shown touching, as in this instance of the

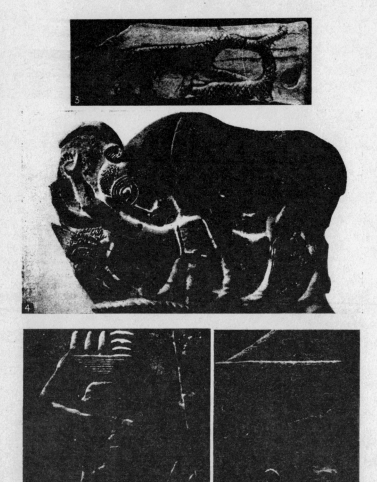

3. Prehistoric
5. Old Kingdom (IV)

4. Earliest dynastic
6. Middle Kingdom (XII)

dog and addax. In short, the figures are mere sym-
bols of ideas, with little regard to their actual nature
and appearance. This symbolic stage of art is found
in most countries, and often with a higher sense of
form and expression than among the prehistoric
people of the Nile; there is nothing of this age in
Egypt to compare with the carvings of the cave men
of Europe.

There is no sign of progress in art during this
time. The slate palettes, cut in the
forms of animal outlines, which were
made through the whole age, begin
with recognisable forms; and these
were degraded by copying, until at
the end their original types could

EARLY. LATE.

hardly be guessed. The animal figures on ivory
combs are passable in the earlier part of the age,
and disappear entirely later on. The human figures,
which are frequent in early times, are very rarely
found later. The flint working shows degeneration
long before historic times. And the pottery loses
its fine forms, regularity, and brilliant finish, and
becomes rough and coarse. In every direction it
seems that the earliest prehistoric civilisation, which
was probably connected with Libya, was superseded
by a lower race, which was probably from the East.

ARTS & CRAFTS OF ANCIENT EGYPT

The first dynasty (5500 B.C.) appears to have brought in entirely new influences. While the material civilisation naturally went on with many of the older elements, yet in all directions a new spirit and moving power is seen. The conquest of the country by a race of invaders is shown on many carvings, most of which are probably of the three centuries of unification, before the start of the dynastic history of the whole country. One of the most typical of these carvings is fig. 4, where the king is represented as a bull trampling upon his enemy. Other examples are given in figs. 51 to 54.

The whole character of the art is changed. Instead of the clumsy and spiritless figures of the prehistoric people, we meet with vigorous forms full of life and character. Perhaps one of the earliest is the hyaena (fig. 51); the slates are rather later, reaching down to the beginning of the first dynasty; and the figures in the round (19 to 22) show what a living and powerful art had suddenly sprung up and was developed under the early kings. The same growth is seen in the advance of glazing for important architectural use on a large scale. And the introduction and rapid development of hieroglyphic writing stamps the new age as the beginning of written history, the start of the conscious preservation by man of a regular record of his past acts.

This new growth of art rejoiced in its fresh found powers. It searched for the truth, it carefully observed anatomy, and—like a learner—it was proud of its knowledge, and emphasised the precise place of the muscles which it had traced out. For that very reason it is essentially a true art, without any of the slovenly substitutes for Nature which are termed conventions. It had no traditions to spoil it or hold it back : it was full of observation as the only method for its work. It is always simple and dignified, and shows more truth and precision than any art of a later age.

After the conscious study of Nature, the greatest step in any art is the deliberate work for the sake of its own beauty, and not merely because it has to tell a story. It may be said that this is the birth of true art ; all before that merely consists of representations for another purpose. But work for the sake of beauty alone is art pure and simple, and this stage was reached at the very beginning of the history, in the beautiful carving of the palm tree and long-necked gazelles (fig. 52).

The Pyramid age (4700–4000 B.C.) brought in fresh ideals. The early kings had expanded a chief·

tainship into a kingdom, without realising all the new conditions of organization which were involved. The great work of the early pyramid kings, Seno-feru and Khufu, was the massive organizing of the civil service of the country, the establishment of a social organism which resisted all the invasions and disasters of the land, and survived in parts to our own times. These new ideals were naturally reflected in the art. In place of tombs such as any great chief might have ordered, the most gigantic pyramids were erected, buildings yet un-surpassed in bulk and in accuracy of workmanship. The new social order of the official world followed in the same lines, and dozens of tombs were sculp-tured in each reign, larger and more elaborate than most of the royal sepulchres of other lands and ages. The host of these tombs which remain constitute a larger treasury of artistic work than there is of any other period in the world's history.

A typical example of this new order is the figure of a servant of a noble named Ainofer (fig. 5). The high rounded relief, the sense of action, the deli-cacy of detail and expression, all mark this new time. The greater part of the really fine sculpture that we possess in Egypt comes from this time. The statu-ary (figs. 23 to 31), the reliefs (figs. 55 to 57), the painting (fig. 68), all show the noble spaciousness and grandeur of the age. Its style is severe and never trifles with superfluities. The smallest as well as the largest work seems complete and inevitable, without being constrained by any limitations of time, or labour, or thought. For the expression of royal energy, dignity, and equanimity the figures of Khufu and Khafra are unsurpassed. In the vivid expression of personal character no age has surpassed the statues of the officials and their wives. The style of other ages may be more scholastic, more amusing, or more graceful, but for all that constitutes great art no period can compare with that of the mighty pyramid kings.

All things pass away, and during the centuries of disruption which followed the VIth dynasty the old style ran down to an incredible coarseness and clumsy copying. At the close of the XIth dynasty a revival took place. Like all great developments of art it rose with extraordinary rapidity, and within a generation or two the new movement was fully grown. Its characteristic was the use of very low relief, with faint but perfectly clear outlines (see fig. 6). It was the style of a school, and not that of Nature. A regular course of artistic training is described by an artist; first was taught the positions of figures in slow action, then the differences of male and female figures, next mythological subjects, and lastly, the attitudes of rapid action. This mechanical training naturally went with elaboration of detail. The minute lining over large masses of hair, the carving of every bead of a necklace, were the outcome of scholastic training. The artificial reduction of figures in the round to a very delicate variation of planes in low relief was according to the same system. The whole works of the XIIth dynasty are beautiful, reserved, and pleasing, with a clearness and finish which appeals to a sense of orderly perfection. They have neither the grandeur of what went before nor the grace of what followed them.

The XVIIIth and XIXth dynasties are the most popularly known age of the art. The profusion of remains, their accessibility at Thebes, and the more intimate style of the designs, have led to their general acceptance as typical. This position must not be allowed in a wider knowledge of the subject. The whole level of art of the XVIIIth dynasty is as much below that of the XIIth, as the style of the XIIth is below that of the IVth dynasty. The scholastic work of the XIIth is followed by a treatment which is almost always conventional in the

7. XVIIIth dynasty   8. XIXth dynasty
9. Saite (XXVI)   10. Ptolemaic

THE PERIODS AND SCHOOLS

XVIIIth; and the XIXth dynasty shows merely a degradation of what preceded it. At the close of the XVIIth dynasty there emerges from the turmoil of the Hyksos barbarism a rude but lively style of drawing, with sculpture of clumsy figures and badly-formed hieroglyphs. Stepping into the XVIIIth dynasty we meet with stiff and rather heavy statuettes, the female figures, however, showing the dawn of the seductive grace which followed. Little can be said to have changed in ideals since the XIIth dynasty, until the Asiatic conquests altered the civilisation of Egypt. Thothmes I and III brought back thousands of Syrian captives, many of whom were selected for their beauty and their artistic ability; their work and their influence transformed the art, and the ideal became that of a light, graceful, fascinating type which posed much and suggested more.

The art of character had become secondary to the art of emotion. Vivacity and romance led the way, and the older studies of deeper life and fine anatomy were out of date. Fluttering ribbons and prancing horses and galloping calves were represented without the laborious sculpture, but merely painted with a flowing line on the tomb walls, which were plastered smooth over the roughest hewing in the rock. The cheapest road to effect was the favourite way, and the eternal solidity and dignified simplicity of the older ages had vanished. The figure of an official of Kha-em-hat (fig. 7) is typical of the best work of this age. The other examples are shown in figs. 36–42, 60–62, 69–78. This new order of things culminated under Akhenaten, when naturalism, influenced largely from Greece, removed the older principles of Egyptian art; and all the passing incidents of life, the domestic affections of the king and the festivities of his court, became the subjects of even funerary sculptures and painting in the tombs. After that stage there was nothing left to do but to fall back on the old stock subjects and copy and re-copy them worse and worse during the succeeding dynasties. Egyptian art perishes with Akhenaten; all that came after was a bloodless imitation.

The XIXth dynasty art is fairly represented by a figure of one of the king's sons (fig. 8). Here is seen the baldness of the style. The profile is mechanical, the hair hangs in a heavy and ugly flap, the body has no anatomy, the legs are badly drawn, and the long streamers flying from the waist are out of keeping. The coarse, heavy work of the temples of Abu Simbel, or the great hall of Kar-

THE PERIODS AND SCHOOLS

nak, is obtrusive in spite of their grandiose conception. In the XXth dynasty the inscriptions also suffered by being cut very deeply, so that the signs appeared as black shadows without any detail. The decay was only arrested by a deliberate copying of the style of the pyramid age.

The XXVIth dynasty tried to recover the early grandeur of sculpture by close imitation, but it is rarely that any fragment of this work does not betray itself by its inane treatment, bad jointing of the limbs, and want of proportion. One of the best examples of the more original work is the figure of an elderly official (fig. 9). The want of detail is hidden by the stiff robe without a fold or curve, leaving only the head and extremities to be represented. Another example is in fig. 64, where the bad jointing and lack of anatomy is too evident.

In the Ptolemaic time these faults are even more apparent, when the bad copy of a copy was the ideal. In fig. 10 is seen the hopelessly wrong proportioning of the parts, the clumsy lumps of flesh and exaggerated muscles, which are the extreme opposite to the over-refined flat relief of the XIIth dynasty. The hair partakes of the same faults, being carved as rows of lumps representing separate curls.

Portraiture, which compelled some attention to Nature, is the latest surviving form of art. In the XXVIth dynasty fairly good heads were occasionally done, but often with some disproportion. The modelled stucco heads of the Roman age are the last stage. Some of them show a real ability and feeling for character (figs. 135 to 137), and one example which can be compared with the skull proves the accuracy of the modelling (fig. 138).

The various Schools of Art should now be noticed. The styles of the different periods that we have considered were of course obvious in all the schools; the character of an age affected all parts of the country. Owing to the absence of any artists' names, and the extreme rarity of those of architects, it is impossible to trace the personal origin of any works. And as we cannot say how much the artists travelled about the country, mere locality does not prove a conclusive test; probably for royal works the artists went to any city according to orders. Among private tombs we can see great differences of style, as between Memphis, Thebes, and Aswan. But the difficulty of exact dating makes comparison doubtful, as we might set side by side works of the rise and of the climax of a period. The most satisfactory evidence about the schools is from the statuary in different materials. When once a sculptor was trained to the peculiarities of one stone he would not be likely to enter on all the difficulties of a fresh material. A man trained for years to slicing and bruising out granite without the least fear of a crack, would not relish hewing soft sandstones that split, or limestone that could not be trusted with its own weight on a finished surface. Certainly the men who learned sculpture on the softer materials would be helpless on the granite. Then we know that the statues were at least dressed into shape—if not entirely finished—at the quarries, and hence the work in one material would continue in the hands of one local school. It is therefore likely that the stone workers of each material formed an unbroken succession, probably in certain families for the most part, and handed on their traditions for several dynasties successively, perhaps even throughout thousands of years. This would not be so much the case in relief sculpture, as there the blocks were built in and sculptured at the building, wherever that might be.

When we look for differences of treatment we see how strongly one style of work is continued in one material through a long period. We have here contemporaneous examples in four different stones, the statues of Rameses II in black granite, hard limestone, red granite and Nubian sandstone (figs. 11 to 14). In all cases work in black granite is finer than that in the other stones at the same period. The figures of the so-called Hyksos type (fig. 34), of the XIIIth, the XVIIIth, the XIXth and the XXVth dynasties, and the sarcophagi of the XVIIIth dynasty, in black granite, all show far finer forms and finish than those in the other materials. Of briefer use there were two other stones which show equally fine work—diorite, which was hardly ever sculptured except in the IVth dynasty (fig. 27), and green basalt, used in the XVIIIth (fig. 37). The green basalt must be put in the highest place as regards minute handling and freedom of curves; the fine grain and moderate hardness were most favourable to the artist. The black granite work comes next in quality, having fine curves but not quite the same freedom, owing to the coarser grain. The diorite has a beautiful grain for work, but the hardness has influenced the detail of recesses, and it is seldom that inner angles are as truly worked out as in the black granite. The comparison is perhaps hardly just, as there are no contemporary works in these two stones. It seems not improbable that all these hard stones were found

11. Black granite   12. Hard limestone
13. Red granite   14. Nubian sandstone

THE PERIODS AND SCHOOLS

in the same region, the Eastern desert, and that they were all worked by one school. That there was a fine technical training there in early times is shown by the splendid bowls and vases of the hardest rocks which were wrought in prehistoric ages and the first dynasty. Such vases were made in the mountain district, as the figures of a warmly-clad race bear them in tribute to the Egyptian king (*Jour. Anthrop. Inst.*, xxxi., pl. xix., 13–15). Thus we may look on this black-granite school as belonging really to the border people of the Eastern desert, and not to the Nile plain.

The limestone school was expressly that of Memphis and Middle Egypt. It is best known from the host of private statues found in the cemetery of Saqqareh. Work of the finest delicacy was done in this soft and uniform material (see figs. 24, 29–32); and a branch of the same school was that working the harder limestones which were a favourite stone in the XVIIIth and XIXth dynasties in upper Egypt, as in the colossus of Rameses II (fig. 12). Both branches of this school excelled in the delicate expression of physiognomy; the proportions of the limbs and the finish of the extremities are usually excellent. The alabaster work is a branch of this same school, with similar proportion and finish. It is a rare material for sculpture till the XVIIIth dynasty, but under Amenhotep II to IV it was often used; and it serves for one of the best works of later time, the statue of Amenardys (fig. 47). The quarries were in the midst of the limestone hills, especially where the hard limestone occurs near Tell-el-Amarna. Thus the same school dealt with this whole group of calcareous rocks.

Another very fine school was that of the quartzite sandstone of Gebel Ahmar, near Cairo. The material was closely limited to a single hill cemented by hot springs; and what is now seen there is only the immense heap of chippings left by workers of all ages: the hill itself has almost vanished. This material was worked in the pyramid times, but only roughly. The XIIth dynasty kings saw its value, and quarried it for sarcophagi and chambers, but seldom used it for sculpture. The XVIIIth dynasty attacked it on an enormous scale; the two great colossi of Amenhotep III, weighing 1175 tons each, were cut and carried up-stream 450 miles to Thebes. Statues are found, royal and private, in all parts of the land, and naturally this stone was largely used at Tanis. The work is usually excellent, almost equal to the limestone sculpture; but it generally falls a little below that of the previous schools in the depth of cutting and the freedom of work in hollows.

The red granite school was at Aswan, where the statues and obelisks are still lying unfinished in the quarries. The artist was much hindered by the coarse grain of the stone, which made fine work difficult. On the obelisks this has been fairly overcome by a great amount of emery cutting, and sharp smooth hieroglyphs were cleanly cut. But for statuary, even in the pyramid age the features are coarsely worked and the detail scanty; and when used later on a large scale, the forms are heavy, the inner angles seldom worked out, and the extremities thick and massive. This is seen in the colossus of Rameses II (fig. 13), as well as in earlier figures.

The Nubian sandstone school was the least artistic. The softness and ready splitting of the stone prevented clean and well-finished work. Detail was almost impossible, and it was a mistake to use a good building stone for the wrong purpose of fine carving. In early times this stone was never used, except locally in its own region. The XIIth dynasty rarely used it, but by the middle of the XVIIIth it became general, and it was the main stone of the XIXth dynasty in Upper Egypt. Its use, however, does not come down to Middle or Lower Egypt. The long avenue of sphinxes at Thebes are the most familiar sculpture in this material, and similar figures were also placed by Amenhotep III in his temple on the Western bank. The great colossi of Abu Simbel are the main example of sculpture in this stone (fig. 14). They show the defects of the other southern school, that of red granite. The limbs are square and heavy, the feet and hands are flat and mechanical, and the muscles are crude ridges. But the face is fairly rendered, as well perhaps as was practicable in such material.

We thus see that there were essential differences between the various schools of Egyptian art, partly due to the various peoples, but mainly resulting from the material used by each school.

CHAPTER III

THE STATUARY

FIGURES in the round are the earliest mode of modelling, and remain the most important, as they are less conditioned than reliefs, and give full scope to ability and knowledge. The earliest human figures are found in the second stage of the prehistoric age, immediately after the white-lined pottery. They are of ivory, limestone, slate, pottery, or of stick and paste. Such figures did not continue to be made after the middle of the prehistoric civilisation. The ivory figures usually end in a mere peg below, with wide hips and shoulders, but no arms. The eyes are marked, though often the mouth and nose are omitted (fig. 15). The limestone or cement figures have the division of the legs lined out; some are standing, as fig. 16, with tatu marks painted on the stone; others are of the armless form, seated, and clearly of the steatopygous Bushman type. The slate figures are always of men, with pointed beards, and white beads inserted for eyes. The pottery figures are roughly modelled, but with the legs separated. The stick and paste figures are made by modelling a vegetable paste over a stick; the legs are marked, sometimes arms are added, or else there are merely shoulder stumps. In one case the head is modelled bald, painted red, and has a black wig modelled over it, showing that separate wigs are as old as the prehistoric time. Some ivory tusks are carved with a much more advanced style of heads (fig. 17), which give the best idea that we have of the type of the people. The animal figures are rudely cut, but have a certain ferocious air (fig. 18).

Some much more advanced figures in ivory have the legs and arms separate, and a passable amount of modelling in the head and body. Though quite of prehistoric style, they are probably influenced by the school of highly developed ivory-work of the Ist dynasty, and may shortly precede that time.

The early dynastic age brought in entirely new ideals. The oldest figures of this time are the colossal statues of the god Min from Koptos. These are of much the same work as the prehistoric human figures, but have spirited drawings of animals in-

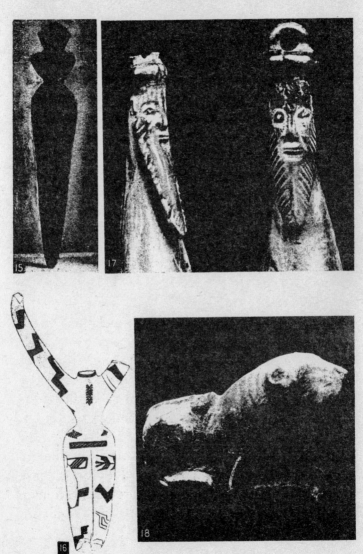

Prehistoric figures in the round

cised on them (see fig. 51). Just before the Ist
dynasty there came a finely developed style of ivory-
carving, which is known to us by the many figures
of men and women found at Hierakonpolis. The
finest stone-work of that age is a study in limestone
of a king's head (figs. 19, 20), which is so closely
like Narmer (fig. 54) that it must be just at the
beginning of the Ist dynasty. It is a sculptor's
study of a king preparatory to making his statue,
and, as Professor A. Michaelis says, "it renders the
race-type with astounding keenness, and shows an
excellent power of observation in the exact representation of the eyes." The delicacy of the facial
curves should be noticed, and the entire absence
of any conventions in the modelling of the mouth
as well as the eyes. The widely prominent ears are
a characteristic of the earliest historic figures ; such
a feature belongs to a hunting race who need to
catch sounds, and suggests that they always slept
on their backs. This is unlike the prehistoric folk,
who were always buried contracted and lying ·on
the side, as being their natural attitude ; but it agrees
with the modern Egyptian, who sleeps in the mummy posture, lying on the back.

A large number of ivory figures were found at
Abydos, fully developed in style, beyond those

of Hierakonpolis. They comprise figures of girls, boys, dogs, apes, a bear, and many lions. They are admirably easy in their pose, and perfectly natural in form with a simplicity and truthfulness better than any later work. The figure of an old king (fig. 21) was with these; notice the subtle expression of the face, the droop of the head forward, and the natural air. This is probably early in the Ist dynasty.

Rather later is the hard limestone head of King Kha-sekhem, of the IInd dynasty (fig. 22). Fine as the modelling is about the mouth, yet convention has already crept in; the edges of the lips are sharpened, and the extended line at the outer corner of the eye has been introduced. We see then under the earliest dynasties the observation of Nature free from any artificial trammels, unconscious, simple and dignified, on a higher plane of truthfulness and precision than is found in later art.

In the pyramid age we will first observe the earlier private figures (23 to 26). Queen Mertitefs (fig. 23) was the wife of Seneferu, at the close of the IIIrd dynasty. In her type of face, and the treatment of it, we see an earlier race and earlier work than that of the pyramid times. The large, staring eyes, the mouth turning down, the natural

19, 20. Ist dynasty king, limestone
21. Ist dynasty king, ivory
22. Khasekhem (IInd dynasty)

23. Mertitefs
24. Nofert
25. Ka-aper
26. Unknown

hair cut short and brushed straight down over the forehead beneath the wig,—all these details disappear after this. When we compare this with the head of Nofert (fig. 24), who was of the next generation, the change of type and work is at once seen. In Nofert the eyes are admirably placed, the brow is perfectly natural, and the modelling of the features is irreproachable. Yet there is less absolute naturalism than in the older work of the Ist dynasty. The hair is evidently kept complete beneath the wig, and is laid out smoothly over the forehead.

The celebrated figure of Ka-aper, or the "Sheykh el Beled," belongs to the same period. The figure is so well known that it need not appear here, but the full face is less familiar (fig. 25). The mouth and chin are perhaps the most truthful part, and seem entirely free from convention. The eyes are excellent in form, but affected by the technical detail of inserting the eyeball of stone and crystal in a copper frame. The similar eyes in the head of Nofert are more carefully inserted, so that the frame is not obvious. The hair is represented as closely cut, so as to allow the wig to be put over it. We can, however, hardly judge of this figure as it is, stripped of the coat of coloured stucco which covered such work. The portions of similar wooden figures in the temple of Abydos had all been thus painted. Such a coat would modify the eye setting, and leave only the dark line visible which imitated the kohl on the eyelids.

Another work of the same age is the best for the pose of the figure (fig. 26). The vigorous, independent, frank attitude is perhaps the finest in any portrait, ancient or modern. The profile is of the same type as that of Nofert, alike in the strong brow and the form of the nose and chin ; the eye is more prominent, and the mouth less luxurious, while the under-chin is firmer. Such differences are all in keeping with the character, that of an active mistress of an estate rather than an easy-going noble.

We shall not find in any of the subsequent work of the pyramid age—still less in the later ages—such vitality and strength of individual character as we have seen in these early portraits. With these stands also the minute head of Khufu (fig. 123), which we shall notice with the ivory-work.

The statue of Khafra (fig. 27) carved in diorite is one of the grandest works of Egypt. The entire dignity and majesty shown contrast strongly with the active air of the subordinate classes. The muscular detail is powerful, but yet in keeping with the serenity of the figure. The whole is best grasped

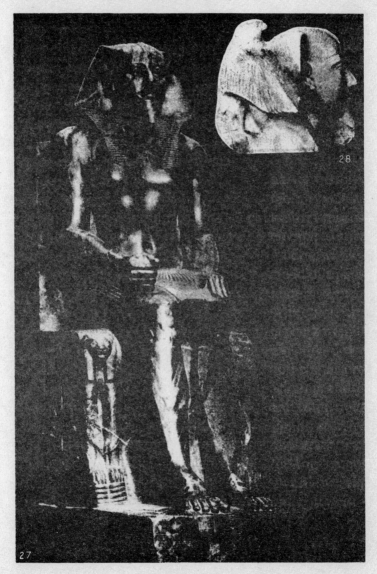

27, 28. King Khafra (IVth dynasty)

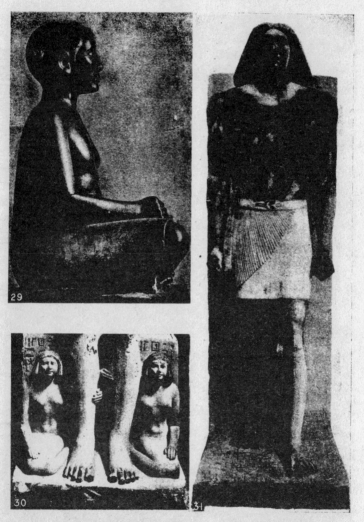

29. The scribe   30. Wife and daughter   31. Ranofer

from below, as it was intended to be seen ; but the head should be studied at its own level, and the profile, from a cast (fig. 28), shows the form as it originally appeared when covered with a facing which concealed the grain of the stone. The difference of character between the calm, easy dignity of this, and the terrible energy of Khufu (fig. 123), should be observed. It shows how free the art is from any mere convention of majesty. The hawk behind the king is shown as spreading out its wings to protect the royal head. This symbolism is ingeniously hidden in the front view, so as not to interfere with the effect of the whole figure as it was intended to be seen. The figures of the Vth and VIth dynasties have more vivacity than those earlier, but scarcely such a real vitality. The well-known scribe (fig. 29) is a good piece of expression, showing the attentive, waiting air of a man who is following dictation. The anatomy is not detailed, and the surfaces look rather blocked out and bald as compared with Khafra.

The lower part of a group is given here (fig. 30) for figures of the seated wife and daughter. These show good modelling of the figure in a close-fitting garment, and the hair is worn over the forehead beneath the wig, as by Nofert. The figure of Ranofer (fig. 31) is one of the most dignified of the portraits of officials. The pose is strong; the muscles are well rendered, and not too full though clear. The wig stands well off the head, and gives a continuous outline with the figure. It is hard to see how the whole expression could be better than this.

On looking closely at the detail of these early statues, there is very little that can be set down as conventional. All the features are natural, well placed, and harmonious. The relation of the brow to the eyes is generally true. But this point was entirely missed in later times. In the XIIth dynasty the eye is rather too forward; and in the XVIIIth there is hardly a single statue that is correct, the eyes usually projecting to the plane of the brow. On observing even the finest figures of later times it will be seen how purely conventional is their treatment; the mouth and eyes are cold and mechanical, and it is seldom that any one feature even approaches the truth of the early art.

In the XIIth dynasty the work shows the scholastic style of deliberate accuracy, without as much personal vitality as in earlier times. Yet it is full of carefully observed detail, and is by no means perfunctory like the later work.

THE STATUARY

The facial surfaces are well rendered : observe the varied treatment of the cheek below the eye in figs. 32, 33, and 35, which are clearly individual. The entirely different form of the mouth in these three is as evidently personal. Throughout Egyptian work the eye is of two distinct types, both of which we see here in the XIIth dynasty. In one type (fig. 32) the upper lid rises to its highest point near the inner side; and with this form the actual corner, or canthus major, may end in a mere angle or in a lachrymal fossa more or less developed, an extreme case of the long and wide fossa being seen in fig. 32, and in the black granite figure from Alexandria (so-called Hyksos) in Cairo. This may be called the gibbous form of lid, and it is the more usual in the sculpture and on coffins. The use of a copper frame round the inserted eye in Old Kingdom statues makes it uncertain how far the lachrymal fossa was intended to appear. But the statues of a single material show a small fossa in most cases, such as Khafra, Dadefra, the (so-called) wife of the Sheykh, and Sebekhotep III. In later work there is no fossa, but only an angle, as in Tahutmes III, Amenhotep III, Amenhotep son of Hapi, and other instances to the end of the dynasties. But a slight fossa is shown in Akhenaten and his family, and in

37

Ramessu II ; and, under the Ethiopians, Taharqa and Amenardys are both shown with a long fossa.

The other type of eye seen in figs. 33, 35 may be called the narrow eye. This seems to belong mainly to the Middle Kingdom, and is seen in Senusert III, Amenemhat III, Queen Nofert, and Noferhotep. It is perhaps unknown at an earlier age; and later it rarely occurs, but may be seen in Merenptah, and somewhat in Mentu-em-hat and some portraits of the XXVIth dynasty. These remarks are merely to draw attention to a detail which is easily observed and seldom defaced; but for drawing conclusions an extensive study is needed of all the varieties of form and treatment, not only of the eye, but also of the lips, nostrils, ears, and hair. How far such detail belonged to the subject, and how much is due to artistic conventions, we cannot yet say ; but from the similarities of portraits of the same person it seems probable that the details are really due to differences of type.

We now have a very difficult question to state as to the origin of the remarkable type of fig. 34. This is one of the class of sphinxes and statues commonly described as being of the Hyksos. Yet, as the Hyksos kings' names are roughly cut on the shoulders of the sphinxes, they are clearly not the

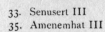

32. Senusert I   33. Senusert III
34. Foreign type   35. Amenemhat III

original inscriptions ; and, as clearly, these figures are older than the Hyksos. The type is distinguished by an extreme muscularity of the face, deeply cut, powerful lips with strong flexures, and the long nose, not very prominent, but broad. All these points are much in excess of such features on any statue of a named Egyptian king. Some similarities may be seen in the type of Senusert III and Amenemhat III (figs. 33, 35) ; but these latter are much less strong and unconventional. It is probable that some of the stock of fig. 34 has gone to form the type of figs. 33 and 35, but it is impossible to see in them a uniform single type. It seems most probable that fig. 34 belongs to an invading people from Syria during the decadence of the Old Kingdom, between the VIIth and Xth dynasties ; but until some example with an original name may be found, it is useless to be more definite. It is noticeable how all of the heads of this type are in black granite, or rarely some other igneous rock ; this suggests that they were wrought by the school of the eastern desert, and may therefore not be controlled by the decadence of ordinary Egyptian work between the Old and Middle Kingdoms.

Whether other strange works in black granite—such as the fish-offerers of Tanis—belong to the same age, has been questioned. It may be noted, however, that the sphinxes and the black granite bust from Alexandria have a large lachrymal fossa, while the fish-offerers have no fossa, but only an inner angle to the eye. The so-called Hyksos figures from Bubastis are not really of this type, but show an inheritance of some of its characters, such as belong to the royal family in the XIIth dynasty. Whenever the royal portraiture of the XIIth dynasty is fully collected and studied, it will be possible to clear the attribution of many statues, and so to separate those which really belong to the earlier stock.

On coming to the XVIIIth dynasty a more mechanical style prevails (figs. 36–39). This is obvious in the formal raised band of eyebrow, and the eyes being brought forward to the plane of the forehead. The lips remain more natural, and are still treated expressively. The best work of this age is the green basalt statue of Tahutmes III in Cairo (fig. 37). It accords closely with another figure of black granite of the same king; but the red granite head in the British Museum is much coarser and less expressive, as is natural from that school of granite work. The large nose is vouched for as a family characteristic in the reliefs of Tahutmes II and Hatshepsut at Deir el Bahri, which have precisely the same outline of brow and nose ; the under-side of the nose, the slightly rising curve of the lips to the outer corner, and the flatness of the facing of the lips, seem to be individual details.

The head fig. 36 is of an official of Amenhotep III, in quartzite. It has a fairly good outline of the cheek, and well-cut lips ; and it shows the more florid and romantic turn of this age in the wavy hair marked out with lines.

Under Akhenaten (fig. 39) there came a revolution of art, which was perhaps only a culmination of the naturalistic tendencies that were growing during the preceding reigns. But it was enforced and supported by the surrounding changes in religion, ethics, and politics which were carried out by the humanist reformer who ruled. It was probably also stimulated by the influence of the contemporary art of Crete and Greece, the whole eastern Mediterranean apparently sharing in a general movement. We shall notice this further when considering reliefs and painting. Of round sculpture the best figure remaining is that of Akhenaten now in Paris (fig. 39). It has been part of a group of the king and queen sitting together, and it shows all the characteristics of this school in the best form. The eyes are quite natural; the lips are emphasised by a sharp edge along their borders; the jaw and neck are excellently rendered; and the ear, with its large pierced lobe, is clearly true to life.

Though the reforms of Akhenaten mostly perished with him, yet the training of his artists is still to be seen in the sculpture of Tut-ankh-amen (fig. 38). This has not the professional completeness of style seen under Tahutmes III (fig. 37), but it carries on the less precise sentimentalism of Akhenaten (fig. 39), with much feeling for expression and beauty, but a lack of grip and force. The brow is neglected, the eye is feeble, the cheek iş without detail, but the lips and chin are enforced as far as possible. The whole effect is sweet but not impressive.

We now turn to the minor work in wood. In the Old Kingdom, wood was frequently carved on a large scale; of the Middle Kingdom there is the statue of King Hor; but under the New Kingdom the only large figures are some rather coarse funeral statues. On the other hand, in small figures there is a profusion of wood-carving. The wooden *ushabtis* are often beautifully treated; the draped figures of women are graceful and dignified, with minute working of the hair and dress; the grotesque figures of toilet objects are full of character; but here our space limits us to one class, and we give

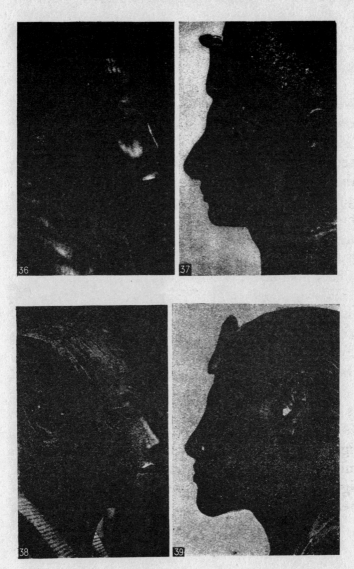

36. Under Amenhotep III   37. Tahutmes III
38. Tutankhamen   39. Akhenaten

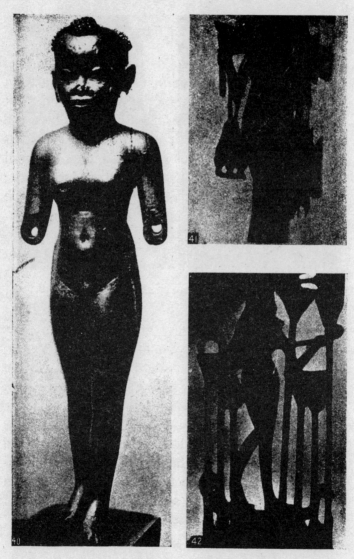

Wood-carvings of girls (XVIIIth dynasty)

the nude figures (figs. 40–42), as such are rarely found in other material.

The little negress (fig. 40), carved in ebony, is part of a group representing her carrying a tray, which is supported by a monkey before her. But these accessories are inferior, and merely hide the figure; the edge of the tray has been slightly cut in on the breast and thus disfigured it. The detail of this statuette is better than any other such work; the perfect pose of the attitude, the poise of the head, the fulness of the muscles, the innocent gravity of the expression, are all excellent.

Other figures are carved in the handles of toilet trays. The girl in fig. 41 holding flowers and birds is on a smaller and coarser scale than the preceding, but is excellent in expression and in the modelling of the trunk. The damsel playing a lute on her boat amid the papyrus thicket (fig. 42) shows one of the graceful adjuncts of water-parties in high life. The length of leg is exaggerated to harmonise with the long stems around; but the pose is skilfully seized, the distance of the feet being needful for balance in a little shallop, while the cling of the thighs is maintained. There is more self-consciousness and deliberate effect in this expression than in that of the little girls seen before.

The age of decadence now begins with the Ramessides. One fine piece arrests us in the black granite statue of Ramessu II (fig. 43), of which an entire view is given in fig. 11. The whole pose is fairly good, the face looking down toward the spectator below. The king is no longer the dignified organiser of the Old Kingdom, with a vision far away beyond everyday matters, but he is obviously considering the opinion of the man in front of him. The detail is almost equal to that of the previous dynasty; the eye is natural, the nose rather formal, the lips with the sharp edge even more developed than before, and the chin and throat less modelled. The elbow is carefully wrought, bringing out the fold of flesh and the muscle separately, the accuracy of which is questionable.

A good example of a private sculpture is the head of Bak-en-khonsu (fig. 44). The eye is only slightly indicated, leaning to the conventional blocking out seen in figs. 91 and 137. The profile is good, and the lips are less exaggerated than in the royal statues. The artist could give all his attention to the face alone, as the figure is entirely hidden in an almost cubic block, which represents the man seated with knees drawn up before the chest.

The head of Merenptah (fig. 45) shows him as

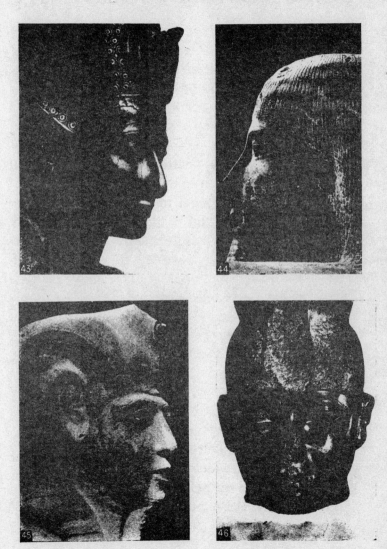

43. Ramessu II   44. Bak-en-khonsu
45. Merenptah   46. Taharqa

inheriting and imitating his father's face and attitude. The style is cold and formal; the eyes are so forward as to be even beyond the plane of the forehead, and scarcely capped by the brow. But the nose and lips are natural and free of the forcing which is seen rather earlier. There is no attempt at any delicacy of facial curves, and the chin and throat are masked by the official beard. As this is in gray granite, and was executed as the *ka* statue of the king's personal temple, it may be taken as the best that could be done at that time.

A different feeling comes in with the massive individual portrait of Taharqa (fig. 46). The facial muscles are strongly marked, but the mouth is singularly unformed, and is exactly the opposite of that in the strong type of fig. 34. The eyes are of the gibbous form, with a long slot of lachrymal fossa, which is also shown in the kindred figure of Queen Amenardys (fig. 47). The style is not akin to any other Egyptian work, and it seems as if an entirely different physiognomy had challenged the sculptor and made him drop his usual treatment and study Nature afresh.

The alabaster statue of Amenardys (fig. 47) is disproportioned as a whole, though parts are good separately. It has just the faults due to an imita-

tor who does not trust to observation. The head
is too large, the jointing is weak. Each of the
features is fairly well rendered; and within the
limits of later mannerism there is no forcing or
exaggeration.

The portrait of Mentu-em-hat (fig. 48) belongs to
the same style as that of Taharqa, and both are in
black granite. The eyes seem too small, but this
is rather due to the depth and massiveness of the
jaws, which overweight the face. The apparent disproportion in the low forehead is only due to the
photograph being taken too close and low down.
The height above the eyes is really equal to that
down to the upper edge of the chin. The facial
curves are carefully observed, and we can well credit
this with being a true portrait of the capable gover-
nor of Thebes who continued in office under Taharqa and Tanut-amen, and who repaired the devasta-
tions of the Assyrian invasion.

A head broken from a statue, found at Memphis
(fig. 49), is remarkable for the deep and searching
modelling. The bony structure, the facial muscles,
and the surface folds are all scrupulously observed.
The artist's triumph is shown in the harmony and
the living character which he has infused into his
laborious precision. Very rarely can a man rise

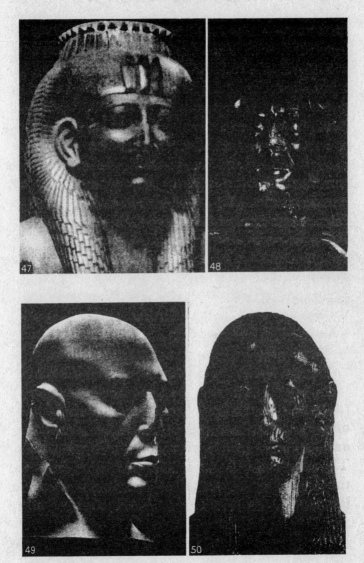

47. Amenardys   48. Mentu-em-hat
49. Basalt head   50. Wooden head

superior to such a rigorous training. The character of work is scarcely Egyptian ; it belongs rather to the same school as the republican Roman portraits, but is earlier than those, as it has more precision of detail.

Lastly, we have one of the best examples of Greek influence in Egypt shown by the wood-carving of a coffin (fig. 50). The long narrow face shaded by thick wavy hair is Greek in feeling, while the feather head-dress is old Egyptian. Unfortunately, the decay of the wood has broken the surface, but it still remains an impressive example of Egyptian influence on art which is mainly Greek.

CHAPTER IV

THE RELIEFS

In reliefs the representation of Nature is complicated by the inevitable use of some conventions, and some kind of perspective, to reduce solid objects to a plane delineation. It follows that for the study of naturalistic art they are inferior to statuary, though they give rise to a whole system of artistic conventions which are of interest in themselves. It appears that among most races drawings precede reliefs, and hence relief must be looked on as developed drawing, and not as trammelled statuary.

The oldest reliefs are those of the prehistoric ivory carvings (see fig. 3), in which we see maintained the pictorial convention of crossing lines to substantiate the outline of a solid body, although the body was now expressed by the relief. A large quantity of ivory reliefs showing rows of animals were found at Hierakonpolis, belonging to the

48

51. Hyaena and bull
53. Group of animals

52. Gazelles and palm
54. King Narmer

earliest historic times. Of the same class are the reliefs upon the primitive figures from Koptos (fig. 51). These comprise the elephant, stag's head, and swordfish, as well as the hyaena and ox. The design is spirited, and seizes the characteristics of the animals; while hills are conventionally shown by lumps under each foot. The method of work is by bruising out the surface with a pointed stone pick around the outline, and so lowering the surrounding ground (here shaded), while the body of the animal remains of the original face of the stone.

The next stage is that of the astonishing slate reliefs. The purely artistic motive is seen in the group of two long-necked gazelles with a palm-tree (fig. 52). The detail of the forms of the joints and the general pose of the animals is excellent, and the feeling for the graceful, slender outline and smooth surfaces is enforced by the rugged palm stem placed between the gazelles. The love of the strange and wild elements is seen in the rout of animals, real and mythical, in fig. 53, which shows the lion, giraffe, wild ox, and many kinds of deer, well known to the early artists.

The figure of King Narmer (fig. 54) is the historical point in these slate carvings. As it is more advanced in style than any of the others, it shows that they all belong to the age just before the Ist dynasty, about 5500 B.C. Here the pose and jointing are excellent, and the muscles are proclaimed by the artist as the results of his observation. The later Egyptian canon is observed that a straight line should pass through the middle of the head, middle of the trunk, point of the backward knee, and middle between the heels : only, as the king is here leaning forward in action, the line is not vertical as it is in later standing figures. The facial characters of the king and his foe are well distinguished ; altogether five different types of race are shown on these early carvings. The surface of the slate has been worked down with a metal scraper, shown by the parallel grooves in the face.

On reaching the beginning of the pyramid age the finest work is seen in the three wooden panels of Ra-hesy (fig. 55, *frontispiece*). The anatomy is full, though not so excessive as in the earlier work. The facial curves are carefully rendered, and the mouth is excellently formed. The eye is of course placed in front view, as it always was by Egyptians. The whole figure has an air of stark vigour, which is fitting to a high official who managed a dozen different offices.

The multitude of the mastaba tomb-chapels of

56. The sacrifice   57. The ox-herd

the pyramid age contain so many thousands of scenes, illustrating every act of life of men and animals, that it is impossible to give any view of their variety. Here we can only give two scenes illustrating composition. In fig. 56 is a group of men dragging down an ox for sacrifice. The arrangement of the lines is clear, each figure stands out separately, the action is vigorous and simple. Another scene of an ox-herd (fig. 57) shows quiet motion, with the unusual turning of the head. This might be thought unnatural, but exactly the same twist of the body may be seen among Egyptians now. This style of relief deteriorated in the VIth dynasty, and then continuously decayed until the middle of the XIth dynasty, by which time it has reached a most degraded state.

Suddenly, in the middle of the XIth dynasty, a new style of careful elaboration begins to appear, a true archaic germ of a new school. This rapidly grew, until at the later part of that dynasty there is a stiff and over-elaborate style, which is well shown in the figure of the princess Kauat having her hair curled (fig. 58). The eyes of all the figures are gibbous, with a moderate fossa; the lips have usually a sharp edge, though sometimes merely rounded; and there is the beginning of facial modelling.

In the XIIth dynasty the surface modelling be-came-elaborate, most delicate gradations being wrought with faint outlines, as seen in the Memphite head, fig. 6. A bold high relief and simpler treatment was followed by the Theban school, as in fig. 59 of the god Ptah and Senusert I embracing. The use of sunk relief, as fig. 58, was as early as the IVth dynasty, though most of the tomb sculptures are in high relief. Sunk relief became commoner in the Middle Kingdom, and almost universal in the New Kingdom. It saved a large amount of labour, and it protected the sculptures from injury; but it is so forcible a convention that it is never so pleasing as the raised work.

The XVIIIth dynasty opens with another revival of art, but yet it never reached the levels of the earlier ages. The profusion of reliefs of Thebes and other great sites has made the style of the XVIIIth and XIXth dynasties the most familiar to us, but its inferiority to that of the previous periods is more obvious the more it is studied. The sculptures of Hatshepsut at Deir el Bahri are celebrated, yet the detail in fig. 60 is not rich. There is scarcely any modelling of face or muscles, mere flat surfaces sufficing; there is but little expression in the features; and the whole effect is flat and

58. Toilet of princess   59 Senusert I and Ptah

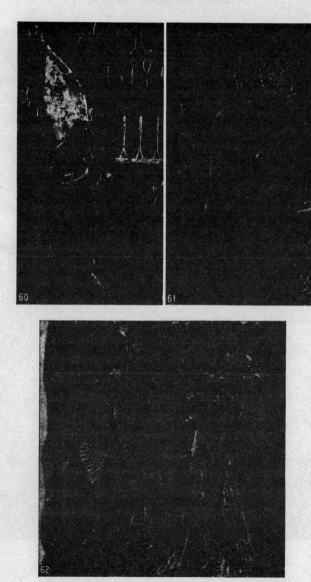

60. Hatshepsut   61. Servant of Kha-em-hat
62. Akhenaten and queen

tame. More character appears under Amenhotep III (fig. 61), though even here there is none of the muscular detail which was constantly shown in early work. The features smile gracefully without any real expression, and the trivial details of dress are worked out to give a picturesque elaboration. The taste for mere prettiness and graceful personalities ruled more and more as the XVIIIth dynasty developed.

At last this taste, stimulated by the influence of the Greek art and its love of expressing motion, broke all bounds in the movement under Akhenaten. The example in fig. 62 gives the essence of Atenism. The natural but ungainly attitudes, the flourishing ribands, the heavy collars and kilt, the ungraceful realism of the figures, the loss of all expression and detail of structure,—all these show the death of a permanent art in the fever of novelty and vociferation.

This ferment being passed, the Egyptian went back on his older style ; but it had lost its life, it could only be copied. The exquisite smoothness and finish of the good work of Sety I at Abydos is entirely lifeless and destitute of observation. It has no anatomical detail, but was made by well-constructed human machines who could not express an emotion which they did not feel.

53

ARTS & CRAFTS OF ANCIENT EGYPT

The historical scenes of the great sculptures of Karnak are full of interest, but almost destitute of art. Some parts of the work of Ramessu III at Medinet Habu show more observation, such as the hunting scene, fig. 63. The wild bulls are well studied, and the marsh-plants with feathery tops show a real appreciation of natural growth and beauty.

Under the XXVIth dynasty came the deliberate imitation of the work of the Old Kingdom. In a few cases this is passably done, and even some invention may be seen. But in general there is only a lifeless imitation of various parts clumsily put together. One of the best pieces of such art is the procession of youths and maids carrying animals and farm produce (fig. 64). The forms are true, there is none of the later exaggeration (as in fig. 10), and there is a loving touch in the details, especially of the animals, which belongs to the true artist. Observe how the girls carry the flowers and the birds, while the boys take the heavy loads of papyrus stems and a calf and a basket of flour. Such work is the last flicker of Egyptian art in reliefs, and nothing later claims our notice.

63. Bulls in marshes   64. Bearers of offerings

CHAPTER V

THE PAINTING AND DRAWING

PAINTING is certainly the earliest art of Egypt; but, being more perishable than sculpture, many periods of it are hardly represented at present. A very early prehistoric vase, painted with white slip on the red ground, shows the crude figures of two men fighting (fig. 65). Other such vases have plants and other objects painted. From the middle of the prehistoric age, belonging to the second civilisation, are the light-brown vases painted in red, with figures of ships and people (fig. 66), plants, and imitations of stone and wicker patterns. The joints are fairly correct in the men and animals, though deficient in the woman with raised arms. But the whole air is very crude as compared with the roughest efforts of the dynastic race. Another painting rather later in the prehistoric age is the ship from a tomb fresco (fig. 67). The arms of the woman are more

55

correctly drawn as straight, but the men are worse posed than in the earlier work. The idea of the figures seen above the ships, but entirely detached from them, may be that they are seen on the opposite bank of a narrow river, beyond the ships.

The advanced painting of the early pyramid times is shown by the geese (fig. 68), stalking along in a meadow amid tufts of herbage. The air of grave self-sufficiency is admirably caught, and this small piece of a great wall-scene at Medum is deservedly admired. Of the Middle Kingdom there is no fine example remaining.

The great age of painting was the XVIIIth and XIXth dynasties. The sculpturing of tombs was then abandoned in favour of the cheaper paint; and the taste of the age for graceful and light treatment found its best scope in the use of the brush. Here we have a group of pelicans (fig. 69) with an old herdsman and baskets of eggs. Next (fig. 70) is a harvest scene. Two men are carrying a load of the ears of corn in a net. Behind are the stalks of straw after the ears have been cut. Two girls who were gleaning have stopped to quarrel over the corn; one has seized a wrist of the other, and the two free hands have each taken a grip of the other one's hair. To the right, under a sycomore fig-tree, one boy

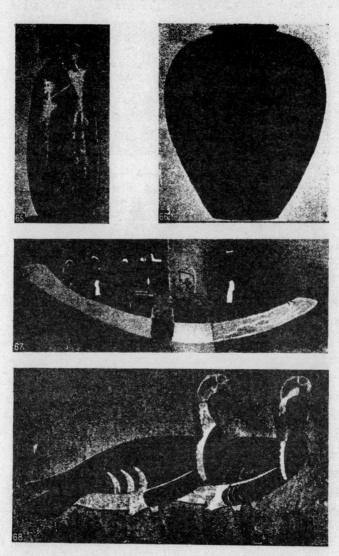

65. First age of prehistoric painting   66. Second age
67. Ship on wall-painting   68. Geese of Medum

69. Pelicans and keeper 70, 71. Harvest scenes

is asleep, while another plays on a long reed pipe, with a water-skin hung over his head. In the lower line a girl with a thorn in her foot is stretching it out to be examined by another girl. Further, a lad is stripping the heads of millet by dragging them through a fixed fork. The whole scene is full of incident, and the drawing of the figures in unusual action is excellent. The curious dress of the men is a linen waist-cloth, with a net of slit leather-work to take the wear, and a solid piece of leather left in the middle of it for sitting on, as in fig. 140. Such slit leather-work is dealt with in the last chapter.

A third scene (fig. 71) is in the harvest field; the ears have been put into a net, and to press them down a stick is passed through a hole on one edge, while a man has hooked his arm over the stick, and jumped up so as to bring his weight with a jerk to press the stick down; with his other hand he holds the end of a cord tied to the net, so as to be ready to secure the stick when pressed down and prevent it springing up again. The spirit shown in this action is very good, and it is perhaps the only figure given in the act of jumping. On the left is a young woman, one of the daughters, behind the owner of the tomb; on the right is a gleaning girl, stopping in the tall corn to drink, with her basket set on the ground.

On the next plate a portion of a ceiling pattern (fig. 72) shows how such designs were drawn. The rhombic lines were done first, then the dark ground-work, leaving white discs, and lastly these were filled up with the spirals. The whole was copied from *appliqué* leather-work, with lines of stitching.

A boating scene (fig. 73) shows the beautifully bold, clean lines of the drawing, for which in this case there does not seem to have been any preliminary sketch of position. The crouching girl picking a lotus bud from the water is very unusual. The drawing of wavy water-lines, with lotus flowers, is the general convention, and the figures of fish and birds are often seen.

A scene at a party (fig. 74) shows the guests seated on the ground holding lotus flowers, while a serving-girl stretches forward to arrange the earrings of one of the guests.

Painting received a great stimulus under Akhenaten : the new movement suited the brush much better than the chisel. The two figures of the princesses (fig. 76) show possibilities which were not then fully carried out. The conventional attitudes are dropped, and the actual positions of two little girls are carefully copied. The elder is seated on a cushion, with the knees drawn up, and resting one

72. Ceiling   73. Boating scene   74. A party

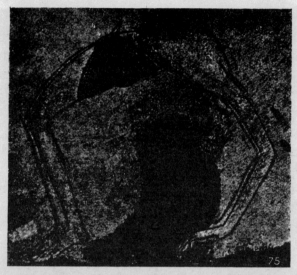

75. Girl somersaulting   76. The young princesses

arm on the knee, while with the other hand she pushes up her little sister's chin. The younger has none of this self-possession, but is propping herself up with one arm, while she clings to her elder's shoulder with the other. The drawing is free and true, within the usual conventions of perspective. Further, the colouring has shade on the backs of the figures, and a high light on the thigh of the younger daughter. Such shade does not appear in Greek art till a thousand years later. The pattern in front is the border of the carpet on which the queen was seated, her foot and drapery appearing above.

A surprising drawing which belongs to the same school of observation is the tumbler (fig. 75). Here an acrobatic position is so skilfully drawn as to suggest its truth and to avoid any impossibility. The form of each part is admirable ; and if we trace it piece by piece into an upright position, the resulting figure is correctly proportioned, except in the length of the arms. In reality such an attitude requires the hands to rest on the finger-tips where the wrist now is drawn. As a drawing of a violent attitude this is a marvellous work, not only for the directness and perfection of the line, but also for the complete lightness and swing of the whole figure.

Another good piece of action is the man (fig. 77)

who is standing on a boat's cabin hauling in a rope. The dead-weight of the body is well thrown back; and as the base is small, one leg is kept in reserve behind so as to recover any slip. The dead pull, with both feet planted together and the whole body rigidly leaning back, is often drawn in the early fishing scenes; but such an attitude would be unsafe when standing on the top of a narrow cabin.

We now turn to outline drawing, in which the Egyptians always had a grand facility. There is no instance, even in degraded times, of an outline made as in modern work by little tentative touches feeling the way. If they made a mistake, they at least "sinned splendidly." The long free strokes, always taking the whole length of a bone at once, and often going down a whole figure without raising the hand—even, true, without a quiver or hesitation—shame most modern outlines. The group of heads (fig. 78) shows well the amount of character given by a simple outline. The furthest is a negro, the next a Syrian, the third an Abyssinian, the last a Libyan. The type of each is shown with zest and energy, and the line-work could not be improved.

In fig. 79 is a very rough sketch for a little tablet of adoration. It shows the faint outlines in red which were laid in first to space out the figure.

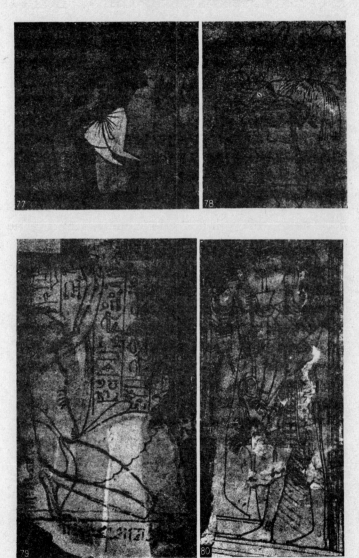

77. The boatman hauling
79. Sketched tablet

78. The four races
80. Tomb decoration

THE PAINTING AND DRAWING

Such were used in nearly all cases as a preliminary guide ; but they were freely improved on in the final black drawing, as here the whole base has been lowered. This also shows the sketch-forms of hieroglyphic writing.

The final work for a royal tomb is seen in fig. 80, Sety I offering to Osiris. We can here admire the perfect freedom and exactitude of the handling, although this was only intended as a guide to the sculptor, and was not to be finally visible.

A large branch of drawing which we have not space to illustrate here is that of the papyri and hieroglyphs. The papyri show the clear, fine outlines in the good examples. In later times, rough as the work may be, the feeling for expression never deserts the artist. The hieroglyphs form a great study by themselves. The sources of the signs, the various treatment of them, the minute details introduced, are all full of interest. The great result was that the Egyptian had a writing which, though cumbrous, was a continual pleasure to see, and which adorned the artistic monuments on which it was placed.

CHAPTER VI

THE ARCHITECTURE

Strange to say, Egyptian architecture has never yet been systematically studied ; we know nothing of its proportions and variations.

The earliest constructions were of brick, or of palm-sticks interwoven. From the necessary forms of these all the details of the stone architecture have been copied. A parallel is seen in Greece, where the architecture was an exact transcription of a wooden building, the triglyphs, mutules, and guttae being the beam-ends, tie-boards, and pegs formerly belonging to woodwork.

For the greater security of the corners of brick  buildings, the Egyptians tilted the courses up at each end, thus building in a concave bed, with faces sloping inwards. This slope was copied in the stonework, and is seen on the outsides of all Egyptian buildings (see fig. 83). The inside faces are always vertical, and this serves to distinguish the meaning of small portions of wall in excavations.

Slight structures were made of palm-sticks, set upright, and lashed to a cross stick near the top, with other palm-sticks interwoven to stiffen the face, and the whole plastered with mud. Such construction is made now in Egypt, and is seen in the earliest figures of shrines. At the top the ends of the palm-sticks nod over, and form a fence to keep out intruders. This row of tops is the origin of the stone cavetto cornice, which always

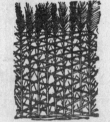

stands free above the level of the roof. At the corners the structure of palm-stick was strengthened by a bundle of sticks or reeds lashed round, and put as a buffer to prevent a blow breaking in the edge. This became the roll with lashing pattern which is seen down the edges of the stone buildings, and also beneath the cavetto cornice where it is copied from the line of sticks below the loose tops (see fig. 83).

Another form of construction was with papyrus

stems. These had a loose, wiry head like an *Equisetum* or mare's tail. When used for a cabin on a boat, the roofing stems were put through the loose

head, which was tied above and below to hold them. Hence the row of heads became copied as an ornament along the tops of walls, and continued in use thus down to the latest times.

The use of the arch was familiar from early times. Even before the pyramid-builders small arches of bricks were made. They were the general mode of roofing in the XIIth dynasty, when we see them drawn and imitated in stone. From the XIXth dynasty there remain the great arched store-rooms of the Ramesseum. Being of dried mud brick, which is far more easily crushed than stone or burnt brick, the circular form was not suitable, as the apex would yield by crushing. A more or less parabolic form was therefore used, so as to give a sharper curve at the top. To protect these arches from the weather, they were laid four courses thick, with a deep layer of sand and gravel over the top, to absorb any rain as a sponge.

Arches were usually built without any centring; and to this day the Egyptian similarly builds arches and domes of any size without centring or support. Each ring of arch is laid on a sloping bed, so that the thin arch bricks on edge will stick in place by the mud-mortar until the ring is completed. The same construction is started in each corner of a room until the arching meets in a circle, when the dome is carried round ring on ring, increasing the dip toward the top. The successive coats of an arch are often bedded on opposite slopes, so that the rings cross each other.

The outer form of a temple was always a blank wall on all sides, as at Edfu, which preserves its circuit wall complete. Usually the outer wall has been removed for building (fig. 83), and the inner courts with columns are exposed. In further ruin all the walls of squared blocks are gone, and only a group of pillars is left on the site.

A typical building of the early age is the temple of red granite built by Khafra at Gizeh (fig. 81).

The pillars are 41 inches square, and there are sixteen of them in the two halls. The work is perfectly plain ; not a trace of ornament is to be seen in this or other temples of the IIIrd–IVth dynasties. Only on the outside was there a panelling, like that on the brick buildings and stone sarcophagi of this age. The masonry of this temple is much less exact than that of the early pyramids. The whole effect of it is grand and severe, with the noble breadth which belongs to the early times.

The tower front of the temple at Medinet Habu (fig. 82) is one of the few façades that is preserved. It was copied from the Syrian fortresses, and shows how the Asiatic influences had entered Egypt during the three centuries from about 1500 to 1200 B.C.

The most complete view of a whole temple is that of Dakkeh (fig. 83). The girdle wall has been destroyed, thus exposing the components of the temple clearly. At the left is the great pylon, the gateway through the girdle wall. This led to the portico, which was the front of the house of the god, like the porticoes to human houses. Behind this a cross passage, of which the door is seen at the side, passed in front of the shrine and its ante-chamber. This was one of the most perfect small temples, but it has been much destroyed in recent years.

81. Granite temple   82. Medinet Habu   83. Dakkeh

84. Palm capital   85. Rose lotus   86. Blue lotus

THE ARCHITECTURE

The massive square pillars of the granite temple gave place before long to more ornamental forms. The principal types are the palm and lotus in the Vth dynasty, and later the papyrus. The palm capital is shown on the granite columns of Unas (fig. 84). It was probably derived from a bundle of palm-sticks bound together and plastered with mud to stiffen them, like the bundles of maize-stalks which are still used for columns. Around the top of it some of the loose ends of the palm-sticks were left with the leaves to form a head.

The lotus capital appears likewise as a shaft decorated with buds around it (fig. 85). In this case the buds are the short, thick ones of the rose lotus, with flowers of the blue lotus put in the intervals under the abacus. But the lotus bud soon became treated as a solid support, and in the capital of the blue lotus (fig. 86) the whole is formed of four lotus buds. The bands of the tie were always strongly marked, however changed the capital might become in later time. The papyrus column belongs mainly to the XIXth dynasty, as in the great hall of Karnak. It was the most incongruous of all, as a single gigantic head of loose filaments was represented as supporting the whole weight.

Plain polygonal shafts were also common. Some

67

octagonal ones occur in the Vth dynasty. In the XIIth dynasty they are sixteen-sided, keeping the four main faces flat and slightly hollowing the others. This was continued in the earlier part of the XVIIIth dynasty, but after that the polygonal form almost disappears.

Here we can only touch on some of the artistic elements; the architecture as a whole is beyond the scope of so small a volume.

CHAPTER VII

THE STONE-WORKING

WE here begin to deal with the more technical rather than the purely artistic view—the crafts as well as the arts. Connected with the last chapter is the study of the materials and methods used for the architecture.

Limestone was the main material of the land, the Eocene cliffs fencing in the Nile valley along four hundred miles. The two finest kinds are the Mokattam stone opposite the pyramids, which is perfectly uniform and free from splitting or flaws ; and the hard silicified stone occurring at Tell el Amarna and elsewhere. The next commonest material was soft sandstone from Silsileh, used generally after the middle of the XVIIIth dynasty, especially in the Thebaid. The less usual stones are the red granite of Aswan, which was used from the Ist dynasty onwards; the quartzite sandstone of Gebel

69

Ahmar near Cairo, begun on a large scale by the
XIIth dynasty; basalt from Khankah and other
eruptions, used in the IVth and XIXth dynasties;
alabaster from the quarries near Tell el Amarna;
and diorite, used by the pyramid builders only.

The quarrying of the limestone was usually by
large galleries run into the best strata. Blocks of
two or three feet in size were cut out by picking a
trench wide enough for the arm to pass downward
around the block, and then inward below it, until
it could be cracked away from the bed. The blocks
were thus cut out in regular rows, from top to
bottom of the gallery face. The same method is
still kept up in the open-air quarry at Helwan. For
larger blocks a trench eighteen inches wide, in which
the workman could pass, was cut around the block.
In the sandstone quarries the same mode of cutting
was followed, only the quarry was open to the sky.
So carefully was inferior stone rejected, that instead
of following cracks in the rock, a wall of stone was
left on each side of a crack; and such walls, each
containing a fissure, divide the quarry to its whole
depth.

The granite was first obtained from loose water-
worn blocks at the Cataract, a great advantage of
such a source being that any cracks are made vis-

ible. Later it was quarried in the bed ; a large mass
still in the quarry has been trimmed and marked
across to be cut up for shrines or sarcophagi. The
early mode of fissuring was by cutting a groove
and jumping holes through the thickness of the
stone, to determine the direction of the fissure.
Probably the active force was dried wood driven in
and wetted, as there is no trace of bruising by
metal wedges on the sides of the groove. In later
times, instead of holes, mere pockets were sunk
rather deeper in the groove to hold the splitting
agent.

For cutting passages or chambers in rock, the
method was to make a rough drift-way, then finish a
true plane for the roof, next mark an axis upon the
roof plane, trim the sides true to the distance from a
plumb bob held at the axis, and finally smooth the
floor to a uniform distance from the roof. In a rock
chamber the roof was finished first, and a shaft was
sunk to the intended depth of the chamber to mark
it out.

The surfaces of rock and of dressed stones were
picked smooth by a short adze, with cuts crossing
in all directions. The edges of a stone were first
dressed true, and then the space between was re-
ferred to the edges. To do this, two offset sticks

with a string stretched between the tops of them were stood on the edges, and a third offset was used to test the depth to the face, so as to see how much was to be cut away. For larger stones, a diagonal draft-line was cut true as well as the edge drafts, so as to avoid any twist. The face was finally tested with a portable plane smeared with red ochre, and wherever that left a touch of red, the stone was cut down; this was continued until the red touched at intervals of not more than an inch. This was the quality of face for joints; but it was further smoothed by grinding on outer finished surfaces. The rough hewing of rock tombs was generally done with mauls of silicified limestone, which is found as nodules left on the surface.

The granite and hard stones were also sawn, and cut with tubular drills. The saws were blades of copper, which carried the hard cutting points. The cutting material was sand for working the softer stones, and emery for harder rocks. As far back as prehistoric times, blocks of emery were used for grinding beads, and even a plummet and a vase were cut out of emery rock (now in University College). There can be no doubt, therefore, of emery being known and used.

The difficult question is whether the cutting material was used as loose powder, or was set in the metal tool as separate teeth. An actual example was found at the prehistoric Greek palace of Tiryns. The hard limestone there has been sawn, and I found a broken bit of the saw left in a cut. The copper blade had rusted away to green carbonate; and with it were some little blocks of emery about a sixteenth of an inch long, rectangular, and quite capable of being set, but far too large to act as a loose powder with a plain blade. On the Egyptian examples there are long grooves in the faces of the cuts of both saws and drills; and grooves may be made by working a loose powder. But, further, the groove certainly seems to run spirally round a core, which would show that it was cut by a single point; and where quartz and softer felspar are cut through the groove floor runs on one level, and as the felspar is worn down by general rubbing, the quartz is actually cut through to a greater depth than the softer felspar. This shows that a fixed cutting point ploughed the groove, and not a loose powder. Also, the hieroglyphs on diorite bowls are ploughed out with a single cut of a fixed point, only one hundred and fiftieth of an inch wide, so it is certain that fixed cutting points were used for hand-graving. There is no doubt that sawing and grinding with loose powder was the general method, but the use of fixed stones seems clearly shown by the instances above.

The large hieroglyphs on hard stones were cut by copper blades fed with emery, and sawn along the outline by hand; the block between the cuts was broken out, and the floor of the sign was hammer-dressed, and finally ground down with emery. Hammer-dressing was largely used in all ages on the hard stones; the blows crushed the stone to powder, and the stunning of the surface was often not quite removed by grinding, and shows as white spots. The hammer was usually of black hornstone, a tough amorphous quartz rock.

The methods of placing the stones in the building have been often debated. The foundations were usually laid on a bed of clean sand, and this enabled the whole course to be accurately adjusted level to begin with. For temples, it seems most likely that the interior was filled with earth as the building advanced; and thus the walls, drums, and architraves could be as easily dealt with as on the lowest course. This plan is successfully used at Karnak in present repairs. But where stones needed to be raised for a pyramid or a pylon, some staging was required. Remains of a massive brick slope still stand against each face of the unfinished pylons at Karnak. This, however, is only the general mass of the staging, and the actual steps for the stones must have been of stone, as brick would crumble to powder if any lifting work was done directly upon it.

For short blocks a cradle of wood was used, of

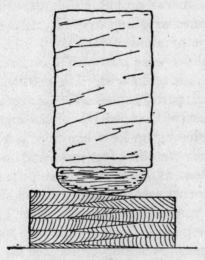

which many models have been found in foundation deposits along with model tools. On tilting this to one end, and putting a wedge beneath it, it could be rocked up the slope, and so gradually raised, first to one end and then to the other. For large blocks, the actual lifting was probably done by rocking up. If a beam be supported by two piles near the middle, a small force will tilt it up clear of one pile; on raising that pile the beam may be tilted the other way, and the lower pile raised in its turn. Thus rocking from pile to pile, a beam can be quickly raised till it is high enough to be moved on to the next step. It was probably thus that the fifty-six granite beams, weighing over fifty tons each, were raised in the pyramid of Khufu.

The obelisks were transported on great barges, as shown in the sculptures. The method of raising such stones is partly explained by an account of setting up colossi of Ramessu IV. A causeway of earth was made sloping up for a length of a quarter of a mile; it was ninety-five feet wide, and one hundred and three feet high on the slope, probably about sixty or seventy feet vertically, as the slopes were held up steeply with facings of timber and brush-wood. The purpose of this evidently was to raise the great block by sliding on its side up the slope, and then to tilt it upright by gravity over the head of the slope. How the mass would be turned we have nothing to show, but probably the simplest way, by gradually removing earth, would be followed. By next ramming earth beneath the obelisk as it lay on a slope, it would be quite practicable to force it forward into an upright position.

THE STONE-WORKING

After a building was finished the sculpturing of its walls had to be executed. For this, a long training of sculptors was needful, and the art schools filled an important part in education. The simplest subjects of outlines in limestone were a first step, the sign *neb* requiring a straight and a curved line only. After the geometric forms came studies of heads and of hands. In fig. 88 we see how, after a fair control of the graver had been attained, there was still much to be learned in detail and harmony before the artist could be trusted to decorate a temple.

Statuary also needed a long training. The work was first marked out in profile of the front and sides, and then cut along these outlines, as in the rock-crystal figure (fig. 89), where the outlines at right angles have been cut, but the corners are yet unrounded. In the block for the head of a lion (fig. 90) the various planes have been already cut for the face, before attempting any rounding. The limestone head (fig. 91) shows a further stage, where the general rounding is done, but the details of the lips, ears, eyes, and eyebrows are yet left in the block. All of these stages needed incessant practice, and years must have been spent in training in the schools before final work was undertaken.

Turning now to stone-work on a smaller scale, the hardest materials were wrought for vases in the prehistoric age. In the first civilisation, basalt, syenite, and porphyry were in use as well as the softer stones, alabaster and limestone. The later civilisation brought in slate, coloured limestone, serpentine, and lastly diorite, which continued to be the favourite stone into the pyramid age. The main differences of form are shown in fig. 87. The earlier type of vase is the standing form F, with a foot, and no piercing for suspension. The later prehistoric age brought in the suspended stone as well as pottery vases. The main types were A, B, D, E, G, H, and lastly C, cut out of coloured marbles, of syenite, and of basalt. All of these vases were cut entirely by hand without any turning, or even any circular grinding, on the outside. The polish lines cross diagonally on the curved sides, and the slight irregularities of form, though imperceptible to the eye, can be felt by rotation in the fingers. The greatest triumph of this stone-work is the vase from Hierakonpolis in black and white syenite, of the type A, E, two feet across and sixteen inches high, which is highly polished, and hollowed out so thin that it can be lifted by one finger, though if solid it would weigh four hundred pounds. The interior of these

STONE VASES

A–H. Prehistoric   J. VIth dynasty
K. XIIth dynasty   L, M. XVIIIth dynasty

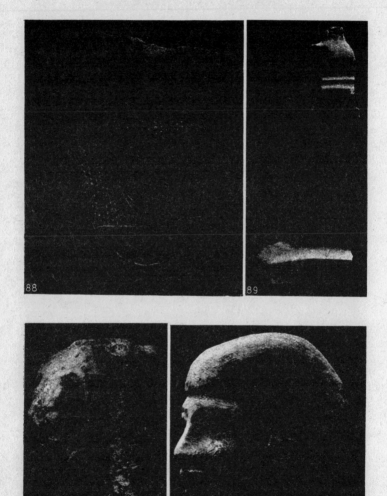

88. Trial piece of learner
90. Lion's head drafted
89. Rough drafting
91. Head nearly finished

vases was ground out with stone grinders fed with emery, and in softer stones cut out by crescent-shaped flint drills.

The historic times show a continual decline in the quality of the stone used. In the 1st dynasty the hard stones decreased, and the softer slate and alabaster were more common. In the pyramid age only diorite continued in use among the hard materials, and that but rarely compared to soft stones; while in the XIIth and XVIIIth dynasties, beyond an occasional vase of obsidian or serpentine, nothing is seen but the soft alabaster. The form J belongs to the VIth dynasty. K is a type which descends from the 1st dynasty, but in this form wide at the top belongs to the XIIth, after which it disappears. L and M are of the XVIIIth dynasty.

Amulets of fine stone were used from prehistoric days onwards. Of the early ones, the bull's head is the commonest, made of carnelian, haematite, or glazed quartz. The fly is made of slate, lazuli, and serpentine in prehistoric times, and of gold in historic jewellery. The hawk is found of glazed quartz and limestone, the serpent of lazuli and limestone; the crocodile, the frog, the claw, the spear-head are all found in prehistoric use. In the Old Kingdom, small amulets of carnelian or ivory were usual; the forms are the hand, the fist, the eye, lion, jackal-head, frog, and bee. In the Middle Kingdom the more usual material was silver or electrum. The New Kingdom used amulets but little; the great profusion comes from the mummies of the Saite time, when dozens may be found on one body. The great variety of forms and materials would require a volume to explain them.

Beads were used from prehistoric times. The hard stones were cut then—quartz, amethyst, agate, carnelian, turquoise, lazuli, haematite, serpentine, as well as glazes on quartz and on paste. Glazed pottery beads became the more usual in historic times; glass beads were made from the XVIIIth dynasty onward, and hardly any other material was used in Roman times. There are hundreds of varieties known, and an accurate knowledge of their dates is essential in excavating.

Flint was worked to the highest perfection in the prehistoric age, and continued in use till Roman times. Strictly, it is chert rather than flint, as the beds in which it is found are of Eocene limestone. But in general appearance and nature they are closely the equivalent of the chalk with flints in England, only harder. The prehistoric forms are shown in fig. 92. They exceed the flint-work of all

Knives and lances of the best prehistoric work

other countries in the regularity of the flaking, the thinness of the weapon, and the minute serration of the edges. At present such work is entirely a lost art, and we cannot imagine the methods or the skill required to produce such results. Besides the weapons, flint armlets were made, chipped out of a solid block, yet no thicker than a straw. These were ground with emery finally to smooth them for wearing. Flint was commonly used down to the XIIth dynasty for knives, but all the dynastic working is far inferior to the earlier. In the XVIIIth dynasty, and later, sickle teeth were still made of flint; and flakes were chipped and used in abundance at some centres in the Roman period.

Before leaving the stone-working we may note the accuracy of work, as this is better seen here than in any other subject. The highest pitch of accuracy on a large scale was reached under Khufu in the IVth dynasty; his pyramid had an error of less than ·6 of an inch on its side of 9069 inches, or 1 in 15,000; and its corners were square to 12″. A change of temperature during a day would make larger errors than this in a measuring-rod. The accuracy of levelling, and of finish of the stones, is on a par with this; joints over six feet long are straight to a hundredth of an inch. The pyramid of Khafra has three times this error, varying 1·5 inch on 8475, and 33″ of angle. That of Menkaura is worse, being on an average 3 inches out on 4154, and 1′ 50″ of angle. At Dahshur the errors are 3·7 on 7459 inches base, and 1·1 on 2065, with angular errors of 4′ and 10′. In smaller work, a beautiful example is the granite sarcophagus of Senusert II, which is ground flat on the sides with a matt face like ground glass, and only has about a two-hundredth of an inch error of flatness and parallelism of the sides. The later ages, so far as we know, have left nothing that can be compared with the accuracy of the early dynasties.

CHAPTER VIII

JEWELLERY

NATIVE gold is, in all countries, one of the earliest materials for manufactured ornaments, and it appears to have been much used in prehistoric Egypt. Though gold is not now sought in or near Egypt, we must remember that it is found in the stream deposits of most countries, and its absence from the Mediterranean lands now is only due to the ancient workers having exhausted the supply. The immediate sources of the metal were in Nubia and Asia Minor. The Asiatic gold was certainly used in the first dynasty, as it is marked by having a variable amount of silver alloy, about a sixth ; but looking at the African influence on Egypt it is probable that Nubia was the first source, though whether gold (*nūb*) was called from the country (*nūb*), or the reverse, is uncertain.

So general was the use of gold for necklaces,

that the picture of a collar of beads became the hieroglyph for gold. Strings of minute gold beads were worn on the ankles in prehistoric times (8000–5000 B.C.). Larger beads were economically made by beating out a thin tube, and then drawing down the ends over a core of limestone. A thin gold finger ring has been found, and a flat pendant with punched dots. But most of the prehistoric gold is seen on the lips of stone vases, overlaying the handles of vases, and forming the wire loops for carrying them. Similarly it was used for covering the handles of flint knives; a sheet of gold was fitted over the flint, embossed with figures of women, animals, twisted snakes, a boat, etc. But the use of thin gold leaf which adheres to its base, is not found until the pyramid times. At the close of the prehistoric period we meet with a gold cylinder seal engraved with signs. When we remember that it is very rarely that an unplundered grave is discovered, the quantity of gold objects found show that the metal must have been generally used in the ages when commerce developed, before writing was known.

On reaching the historic times we obtain a good view of the production and variety of jewellery, in the four bracelets of the Queen of Zer, early in the first dynasty, 5400 B.C. These bracelets (fig. 93) show how each separate piece was made to fit its own place in a complete design, and that the later custom of merely stringing ready-made beads was not then followed.

The bracelet of hawks has the gold blocks alternating with turquoise. The hawks on the gold pieces are all equal, but the sizes of the blocks vary in the height. This is due to their being all cast in the same mould, which was filled to varying amounts. The surfaces were hammered and chiselled, but not either ground or filed. The order of the hawks was marked by numbering them with cross cuts on the base; these cuts are directly across for the blocks on one half, and diagonally across for the other half.

The bracelet with spiral beads has the gold spiral formed of a hammered gold wire, thicker at the middle, where it forms the barrel of the beads. This form is imitated in the three dark lazuli beads down the middle. The triple gold balls, on either side of those, are each beaten hollow and drawn into a thread-hole left at each end; so perfectly wrought are they that only in one instance does the slightest ruck of metal remain. To join the three balls together they were soldered, but without leaving the least excess or difference of colour.

In the lowest bracelet the hour-glass-shaped beads are of gold, with one of amethyst between each pair. The gold is doubtless cast, being solid. None of these are pierced, but they were secured by tying round a groove at the middle of each bead. There was also a fourth bracelet with a ball and loop fastening which shows the skill in soldering. The ball is beaten hollow, leaving about a quarter of it open ; inside it a hook of gold wire is soldered in without leaving the smallest trace of solder visible. The band round the wrist was formed of very thick black hair plaited with gold wire, which was hammered to exactly the same thickness. We see from these bracelets that casting, chiselling, and soldering were perfectly understood at the beginning of the monarchy.

Of about the Ist dynasty there are also copies of spiral shells made by pressing gold foil, perhaps over shells. These were threaded as a necklace, imitating the shell necklaces of earlier ages.

On coming to the VIth dynasty (4000 B.C.) we see gold chains (fig. 94) made of rings, each folded into a double loop and put through the next; these may be called loop-in-loop chain. Gold seals (fig. 95) are also found, probably made by foreigners and worn as buttons, like many similar stone buttons.

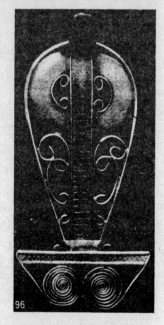

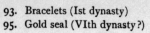

93. Bracelets (Ist dynasty)   94. Chain (VIth dynasty)
95. Gold seal (VIth dynasty?) 96. Gold uraeus (XIIth dynasty)

JEWELLERY

The XIIth dynasty has left us some magnificent groups of jewellery, which were found at Dahshur. The general effect of this work is graceful and sincere in design and pure in colour. There is no glitter and pomp about it, but it has the highest beauty of careful harmony and perfect finish. The tints of the carnelian, turquoise, and lazuli which are used have been precisely chosen for their clear strength of colour, while the Egyptian system of putting a line of gold between two bright colours prevents any dazzling or clashing. The charm of this jewellery lies in the calm, fresh, cool colouring with the unhesitating perfection of the work, which seems to ignore all difficulty or compromise.

Three pectoral ornaments made in successive reigns are each formed of an open-work gold plate, engraved on one side and inlaid with coloured stones on the other. The engraved sides of two are here given (figs. 97, 98), as they are better suited for illustration. The earlier pectoral, bearing the names of Senusert II, is by far the better in design. The scheme of the whole is grasped at once, and rests the eye; there is repose and dignity in it. Although clear open spaces are left, the parts are sufficiently connected for strength.

The second pectoral, of Senusert III, is too complex for a single piece of jewellery for the breast. The heavy mass of the vulture at the top over-weights the design; the head-dress of the royal sphinxes is too tall; and the combination of four captives between the eight legs of the sphinxes, or twenty-four limbs in action, is far too complex and distracting. But in the detail we must admire the expression of the captives; and also the skill with which the parts are united, especially where the frail length of the tails is held in by the extra lotus flowers.

The third pectoral, of Amenemhat III, is the least successful in design. It is made too large in order to take in whole figures of the king fighting; the action is violent; and, not content with four figures, the outlines are lost in a maze of emblems which fill all the space around, so that nothing is clear or restful to the eye. The earliest pectoral was evidently designed to be seen at a respectful distance on royalty in movement. To see the last design the queen would need to be closely stared at, in order to make out the cumbrous historical document on her breast.

Two crowns of gold and inlaid stones belonged also to the princesses. The floret crown (fig. 100) is perhaps the most charmingly graceful head-dress

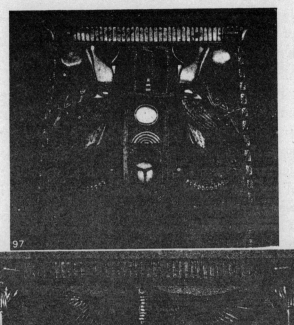

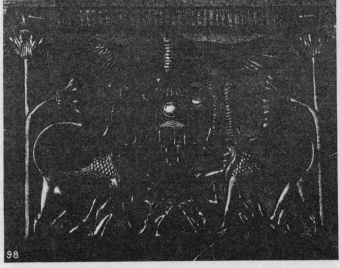

Chased gold pectoral ornaments (XIIth dynasty)

ever seen; the fine wavy threads of gold harmonised with the hair, and the delicate little flowers and berries seem scattered with the wild grace of Nature. Each floret is held by two wires crossing in an eye behind it, and each pair of berries has likewise an eye in which the wires cross. The florets are not stamped, but each gold socket is made by hand for the four inserted stones. The berries are of lazuli. In no instance, however small, was the polishing of the stone done in its cloison; it was always finished before setting.

The upper crown (fig. 99) is less unusual. The motive is the old one seen on the head-dress of Nofert (fig. 24); but the flowers have become conventionalised. The band form is broken by the upright flowers rising from each rosette; and in front there was an aigrette of gold with flowers formed of coloured stones.

Turning now to the technical details, some small gold lions were cast, but not all from a single mould. They seem to have been modelled in wax, and after forming the mould around the model the wax was melted out, and the metal run in. This method, known as *cire perdue*, was usual in later periods. The details are slightly chiselled upon the gold.

Moulding by pressure was used in making cowry beads and tie beads, which were impressed in stout foil, aided by burnishing on to the model so as to tool the detail.

Soldering was done most delicately for the side joints of the hollow cowry beads; it was also used on a large scale for the dozens of delicate ribs of gold which were fixed to the back plates for the cloison work of the pectorals. To attach this multitude of minute ribs exactly in place shows most practised work, for they could not be treated separately, being so close together.

Wire was made in large quantity for the floret crown. This wire was all cut in strips, and pieces soldered together to form a length. The same method was later used by the Jews: "they did beat the gold into thin plates and cut it into wires" (Ex. xxxix. 3). Drawn wire has not been found in any ancient work. A favourite style of work for figures of gods and sacred animals in this age was a mixture of wirework and sheet metal; such amulets and sacred animals are usually half an inch high: the example of the sacred cobra here shown (fig. 96) is by far the finest known.

A new decoration which first appears in this age is that of granulated work (fig. 101). Here it is

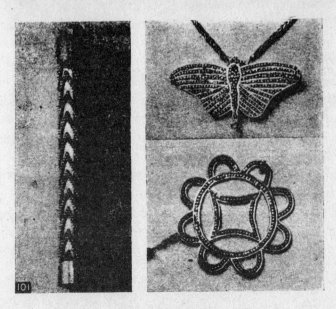

99, 100. Crowns of gold inlaid with stones
101. Granulated gold work (all XIIth dynasty)

seen on a case in a zigzag pattern, and on two pendants. Another example is a pattern of small rhombs
on the bezel of a ring. The granules are 5×5 in
each rhomb, and eight rhombs on the bezel, or forty
granules in about six-tenths of an inch ; allowing
for spaces, the granules must be an eightieth of
an inch wide. This kind of work is found also later
on in Egypt, but it may not be native ; in Etruria it
was the national type of jewellery about three thousand years after this.

The mode of fastening the necklaces was by
grooved pieces. One of the gold cowries, or lion's
heads, or ties which formed the necklace, was made
in two halves with dovetail groove and
tongue fitting into each other along the
whole length of the piece. The tongue ran up
against a butt end when the halves coincided.

When we reach the XVIIIth dynasty we see in
the jewellery of Queen Aah-hotep (1570 B.C.) much
the same system of work as in the XIIth dynasty.
The whole style is less substantial, exact, and dignified ; both in design and execution it is at all
points inferior to the previous work. One new art
appears, the plaiting of gold wire chains, in what is
now commonly called Trichinopoly pattern. This
method was continued down to Roman times.

The Aah-hotep-Aahmes bracelet (fig. 102) is a broad band of metal, with the figures in raised gold on a dark blue ground. At first it looks as if enamelled, as the ground runs in the small intervals between the gold; but it is really a surface formed of pieces of dark lazuli, cut approximately to the forms and patched around with a dark blue paste to match it. Two other bracelets (or perhaps anklets) are formed of minute beads of stones and gold threaded on parallel wires, forming a band about $1\frac{1}{2}$ inches wide. The pattern seems an imitation of plaiting, as each colour forms a half square divided diagonally. The necklace of large gold flies is heavy, and lacks the grace of earlier times. The axe of Aahmes (fig. 104) is beautifully inlaid with gold, bearing the king's names, the figures of the king smiting an enemy, and the gryphon-sphinx of the god Mentu. The dagger (fig. 103) has more of the Mykenaean Greek style in the inlaying of the blade, with figures of a lion chasing a bull, and four grasshoppers. The four heads which form the pommel are unlike any other Egyptian design; but the squares divided diagonally on the handle are like the patterns of the bead anklets, and are probably of Egyptian source.

Of the XIXth dynasty there is the Serapeum

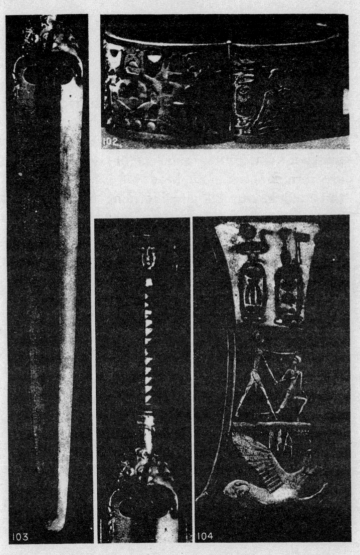

102. Bracelet   103. Dagger (both parts)   104. Axe
(all of King Aahmes, XVIIIth dynasty)

JEWELLERY

jewellery, found with the Apis burials. The pectoral of Ramessu II (fig. 105) is of good design; the wings of the vulture are boldly spread in wide curves, and the king's name is simple, without titles, and well placed. The border band is heavy, and the colouring is rich. It is a creditable work, but entirely missing the grace and sense of perfection of the best work from Dahshur.

The gold bracelets with name of Ramessu II found at Bubastis, are of inferior work, probably for one of his fifty-nine daughters. The name is only impressed on stout foil, which is set in a framework of the bracelet, but the surfaces are ornamented with gold granular work, showing that such was commonly used. There is a pair of collar fasteners, clumsily made by filing the bent gold and working thread-holes in the cut; there are thirty-six thread-holes, so the collar must have been a very wide one. The fastening by two halves sliding together is made by two wires soldered in to form the dovetail. In this same group are thick wire bracelets of silver, with a coarse hatched pattern on the ends; also many plain silver earrings, such as were worn by the common people of this time.

Slightly later is the jewellery of Sety II and

Tausert from the Kings' Tombs. Here are also solid wire bangles, but of gold. And square wire bangles have the thin tail of each end of the bar twisted round the stem on the other side, a fastening also commonly found on finger-rings, of this age and rather earlier. Some clumsy little open-work beads are made by rough circles of gold wire soldered together; a wide equatorial circle is joined to a small polar circle at each end by six small circles touching. Flowers are made by stamping the petals out of foil; there are ten petals to each, and four of them are stamped with the king's name. Some monstrous earrings overloaded with ornament belong to the end of the Ramessides (fig. 106).

Base gold was much used at the close of the XVIIIth dynasty, and many of the finger-rings of that age almost verge into copper. But stones were used for inlay work until the later Ramessides, and glass or paste does not become usual till up to 1000 B.C. Enamel fused upon metal is not known until Roman times.

In the VIIIth century B.C. gold working was well maintained, as seen (fig. 107) in the statuette made by the local king Pafaabast. The modelling of the limbs is exact, the pose is free, and it shows the maintenance of a good tradition. About a century

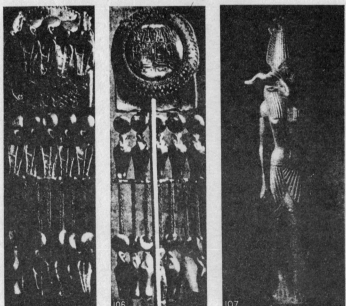

105. Pectoral of Ramessu II

106. Earrings of Ramessu XII   107. Gold statuette (XXVth dynasty)

JEWELLERY

later there is fine cloison work on the gold birds of the Hawara amulets, as minute as any of earlier times.

A free use of gold-work comes in with the wealth of the Ptolemaic age, especially for bracelets and chains. A usual type of bracelet, in gold or silver, was with busts of Serapis and Isis on the two ends of a strip, which were turned up at right angles to the circle. These are generally of coarse work. Plain bangles, bracelets with the two tails of a bar twisted each round the other, coiled wire bracelets which were elastic, and hingeing bracelets, are all found in use at this age. Much Greek influence is seen in the patterns, both now and in the Roman period. The bangle bracelets were often made hollow, both for lightness and economy of metal. Cheaper styles were of thin gold foil worked over a core of plaster; the decoration of cross lines on such shows that they are probably Roman. The chains of Ptolemaic and Roman age (fig. 109) are simple, but of pleasing style.

In Coptic times bracelets of various forms were made, mostly of silver and baser metal; but they are all plain and tasteless. Large earrings were made with a big hoop and a bunch of small pendants, or an openwork metal bead. Necklets of silver were usual, with the tails of the strip wound round each other, so as to slide open for passing over the head.

Gold was also used largely for gilding both metals and wood. The gold leaf was often about a 5000th of an inch thick, weighing one grain to the square inch. Thus a pound's weight of gold would cover about six feet square ; and the gilding of doors and of the caps of obelisks as described is not at all unlikely.

Silver was known to the Egyptians later than gold, as it is called " white gold " ; and it was scarcer than gold in the early ages. Of the prehistoric time there is a cap of a jar, and a small spoon with twisted handle. A few silver amulets are known in the XIIth dynasty. In the XVIIIth dynasty silver became commoner, as the source in northern Syria which supplied the Hittites became accessible. The silver dishes of this age are rather thick, and not finely beaten. One bowl, probably of Ramesside date from Bubastis, has the brim turned inward like a modern anti-splash basin (fig. 115). It seems to have been made by spinning the metal, as thin vessels are now wrought.

The most elaborate style of silver work is that of the bowls from Mendes (fig. 108). These are entirely made by hammer work, and no moulds or

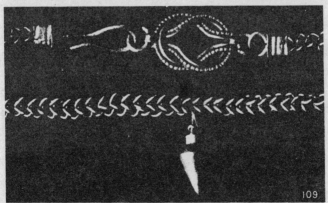

108. Silver bowls   109. Roman gold chain

matrices were used for the forms. But the finish of the surfaces is so fine that no trace of hammer or polishing is left. The design is derived from the fluted vases and bowls of the XVIIIth dynasty; the fluting was made deeper and stronger, and it was suppressed below, as it interfered with the using of the bowl, while round the sides it remained as deep bosses. The detail was all put in by the graving tool, the sinking round the central rosette, the hollows in the petals, and the outlines of the petals. There is no sign of punch-work. The number of ribs is, curiously, indivisible, being 18, 26, 28, and 30; these show that it was not divided either by triangles, hexagons, or repeated halving. Probably a suitable size of rib was designed, and then repeated an even number of times; and the divisions not being truly radial, show that eye-design was followed rather than geometrical scaling.

CHAPTER IX

METAL WORK

HERE we shall deal with the useful metals, apart from the ornamental work of jewellery previously described. Copper was worked from the beginning of the prehistoric civilisation. In one of the earliest graves a little copper pin was found, used to fasten over the shoulders the goat-skin, which was worn before the weaving of linen. Not long after, a small chisel appears, then an adze and harpoon, then needles, and larger sizes of tools come at the close of the prehistoric age. All of this copper was shaped by hammering. Polished stone hammers were used, and the work was so exquisitely regular that a polished surface still remains on an adze, which shows no trace of the method of manufacture; certainly it was not ground. The mode of hammering is shown in some early historical sculptures; a stone hammer was held in the palm of the right hand, which was swung overhead, and brought down on the metal. How such work could be done without hurting the hand by concussion is not clear to us. It is strange that down to Greek times the Egyptians never used a long handle to a hammer.

In the beginning of the kingdom, copper ewers and basins were made; these are known from the sculpture of Narmer, and examples are found in the royal tombs. They were skilfully hammered out, with cast spouts inserted. The main example of early copper-work is the life-size statue of King Pepy, and the smaller figure of his son (fig. 110). The trunk and limbs are of hammered copper, riveted together; the face, hands, and feet are cast doubtless by *cire perdue*. The ease and truth of the whole figure shows that there must have been long practice in the artistic working of copper; yet no traces of such figures are found earlier, nor for over a thousand years later, and we may thus realise how scattered are the points we have, in the view of the art as a whole.

The IXth dynasty has left a coarse example of cast copper tooled with a graver, the brazier of Khety, now in Paris. Of the XIIth dynasty there is not much copper work, except for tools. The moulds for casting tools were found at Kahun.

They were open moulds, cut out of a thick piece of pottery, and lined smooth with fine clay and ash.

Down to this age copper was used with only small amounts of hardening mixture ; after this, bronze of copper and tin came into general use. The earlier copper of the Ist dynasty usually contains one per cent. of bismuth, and later than that one or two per cent. of arsenic, and is "underpoled," in modern terms, that is, a good deal of unreduced oxide of copper is left in the metal. Both of these mixtures harden it ; and by strong hammering it is made still harder. Copper so treated at present can be made as hard as mild steel. Thus the metal was fit for the wood-cutting tools, and for the chisels used for cutting limestone. The harder stones were worked with emery.[1]

Bronze has been found in one case as far back as the IIIrd dynasty, but this was only a chance alloy. It began to be regularly used in the XVIIIth dynasty, 1600 B.C. ; and the source of the tin for it is a point of interest in early trade. Cornwall and the Malay States are the only modern sources of im-

[1] The earlier source of copper was Sinai, where there yet remain thousands of tons of copper slag in the Wady Nasb. In the XVIIIth dynasty and onwards, Cyprus—the Kupros island of copper—came into regular connection with Egypt, and probably supplied most of the metal.

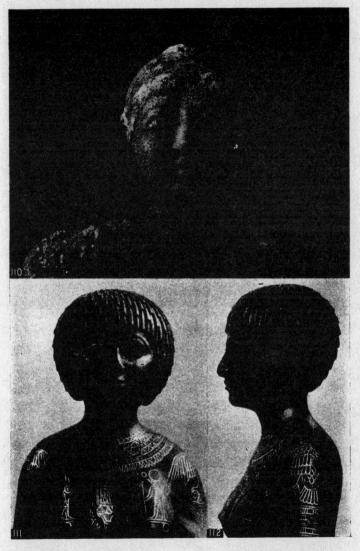

110. Merenra (VIth dynasty)   111, 112. Takushet (XXVth dynasty)

113. Bronze pouring vase   114. Bronze fluted vase
115. Silver anti-splash bowl

portance ; but probably other surface sources have been exhausted, as in the case of gold deposits. Now bronze is found in Central Europe about as early as in Egypt, and it is unlikely to have been imported there from Egypt, or to have been traded there as soon as it would be to a great state like Egypt. The presumption would be that it originated about Central Europe. As a district in Saxony is known as Zinnwald, and crystallised oxide of tin is still brought from there and from Bohemia, it is very likely that there may have been stream tin deposits capable of supplying Europe and Egypt.

In the XVIIIth dynasty bronze vessels were wrought very skilfully by hammer-work. The flask (fig. 113) for washing the sandals of Amen, inscribed with the owner's name and titles, is 9 inches high and has a body 4 inches across; it has been hammered on anvils introduced through the neck, which is only $1\frac{1}{4}$ inches wide. By the weight of it (7 ounces) it cannot average more than $\frac{1}{40}$th inch in thickness. A general mode of stiffening the thin metal vases was by fluting the surface (fig. 114), a method also used in prehistoric Greece.

The casting of bronze was generally done by the *cire perdue* method. A core of blackened sand is usually found in the casting. This was probably sand mixed with a little organic matter; as it is never reddened, probably no clay or mud was used. Over the core the wax was modelled, and the traces of the modelling tool can be seen clearly on unfinished bronzes. On an ibis there was a rolled pellet of wax put between the beak and the breast, so as to induce the flow of the metal along the beak; this would be easily cut away in finishing. An example of a kneeling figure shows the legs completely modelled before putting the pleated dress over them, and then the whole was cast. How the core was fixed within the outer mould is a difficult question. On the many unfinished bronzes that I have examined I have never found a definite connection above the base, but only casual blowholes. Yet the metal was often run as thin as $\frac{1}{50}$th inch, so that a shift of the core by as little as $\frac{1}{100}$th inch would throw the casting out, and make a flaw. How the core was retained so firmly in position against the flotation of the melted metal is not clear. No metal bars were put through the core to steady it, as Cellini did in his large castings. A system was used of stiffening bronze-work by casting it over iron rods; by the free use of iron, this must be of the Greek period. Solid bronze castings come into use in Ptolemaic and Roman work.

METAL WORK

A favourite decoration of copper-work in later times, from about 700 B.C., was by inlaying lines of gold or silver in it. This is a common system in India now, where it is known as *Keft* work; the name suggests that it was introduced from Egypt, where Keft was the starting-point of the Indian trade route from the Nile. One of the finest examples of this is the statue in the Athens Museum (figs. 111, 112); another is the hawk-head and collar with the name of Aahmes II in the British Museum. The lines were first chiselled or punched in the copper, and then the gold was beaten into the grooves.

No instance of using soft solder to copper or bronze is known till Roman times.

Lead is found in the prehistoric times in the form of small figures and little objects; it was probably brought from Syria. It next appears as a rather common metal in the XVIIIth dynasty, when net-sinkers were generally made by bending a piece of sheet lead round the edge lines of the net, much as at the present day. In the filling of bronze weights it is found both in the XVIIIth and XXVIth dynasties. And an alloy of copper and lead—now known as pot-metal—was commonly used for statuettes in Greek and Roman times. In Coptic times pewter bowls and ladles were made; the bowls are apparently formed by spinning.

Tin is first known in a piece of bronze rod from Medum, of the IIIrd dynasty. But this was only a freak, and bronze did not come into use till about 1600 B.C., probably introduced from Hungary, as we have noticed. At about 1400 B.C. there is a finger-ring of pure tin, known by its crackling when bent. The metal is, however, scarcely known separate otherwise.

Antimony occurs in the form of beads about 800 B.C.; as it was familiar to the Assyrians also, it may have been traded from them.

Iron working is an important subject in the history of culture, and the appearances of this metal in Egypt are curiously sporadic. The notion, often suggested, that it might rust away and disappear, is absurd; nothing is more permanent and noticeable than iron rust. The early examples are: (1) a piece of sheet iron said to be found between the stones of Khufu's pyramid; (2) a lump of iron found wrapped up with copper axes of the VIth dynasty form, and placed at the corresponding level in the foundations of the Abydos temples; this is absolutely certain and not open to any doubt; (3) iron ferules said to be found in the masonry of a pyramid at Dahshur; (4) an iron falchion said to be found beneath the base of a statue of Ramessu II. The certainty about the second example—which was found by trained workmen, levelled at the time, and is stuck together with tools of known date— prevents our needing to hesitate about accepting the less precise authentication of the other examples.

Yet iron continued so scarce until about 800 B.C. that we find then a thin iron knife with a handle of bronze cast on it as being the cheaper metal. The explanation of this intermittent use of iron lies in an observation of Professor Ridgeway's, that all the sites of native iron in the world are where carboniferous strata and ironstone have been heated by eruptions of basalt, and thus produced iron by natural reduction of the ore. Exactly this combination is found in Sinai. Carboniferous sandstone has beds of pure black haematite with it, and a thick flow of basalt has extended over the country. Probably, therefore, occasional pockets of native iron were found there by the Egyptians at long intervals, and thus the use of it was intermittent.

The artificial production of iron seems to have been known earliest in Assyria; it probably arose among the Chalybes at the head of the Euphrates, from whom the Greek name of the metal was derived. Large quantities of iron and steel tools have been found in the Assyrian ruins, but were neglected by excavators. A set of armourer's tools was found at Thebes with a copper helmet of Assyrian form, and therefore probably left by the expedition under Asshur-bani-pal in 666 B.C. These tools comprise flat chisels, mortise chisels, saws, a punch, a rasp, a file, a twist scoop, and two centre-bits. The forms of most of these tools have already attained to the modern types; but the file is only slight and irregular, and the centre-bits are only fit for hard wood. The edges of these tools are of steel, probably produced by case-hardening the iron.

We next find iron tools brought in by the Greeks at Naukratis. Chisels, flat and mortise, with both tang and socket handles, borers and axe-heads, were all familiar to the Greek before the Egyptian adopted them. One instance of an iron adze of Egyptian type is known, but otherwise it is not till Coptic times that we find a free use of iron for knives, chisels, flesh-hooks, hoes, pruning hooks, and other tools, probably due to Roman influence. To go further in this subject would lead into the general history of tools, which is beyond our scope here.

CHAPTER X

THE use of glazing begins far back in the prehistoric age, some thousands of years before any examples of glass are known. Glaze is found on a quartz base as early as on a pottery base; and it seems probable that it was invented from finding quartz pebbles fluxed by wood ashes in a hot fire. Hence glazing on quartz was the starting-point, and glazing on artificial wares was a later stage. Amulets of quartz rock are found covered with a coat of blue-green glaze; a model boat was made of quartz rock in sections, glazed over, and united by gold bands; and a large sphinx of quartz, about eighteen inches long, has evidently been glazed. The fusion of glaze on the stone partly dissolves the surface; and even after the glaze has been lost its effect can be seen by the surface having the appearance of water-worn marble or sugar candy. This system of glazing on quartz was continued in historic times ; clear crystal beads flashed over with a rich blue glaze are found in the XIIth dynasty ; and large blocks were glazed in the XVIIIth dynasty.

The use of a pottery ware for covering with glaze begins with beads of blue and green in the prehistoric necklaces. The pottery base for glazing is never a clay in Egypt, but always a porous body of finely-ground silica, either sand or quartz rock. This was slightly bound together, but the whole strength of the object was in the soaking of glaze on the outer surface.

An astonishing development of glazed ware came at the beginning of the monarchy. A piece of a vase (fig. 116) with the name of Mena, the first king of Egypt, is of green glazed pottery, and it is surprising to find the royal name inlaid in a second coloured glaze, which has probably been violet, though now decomposed. Thus two-colour glazing in designs was used as early as 5500 B.C. And at this date glazing was not only a fine art, it was used on a large scale for the lining of rooms. Tiles have been found about a foot long, stoutly made, with dovetails on the back, and holes through them edgeways in order to tie them back to the wall with copper wire. They are glazed all over with hard

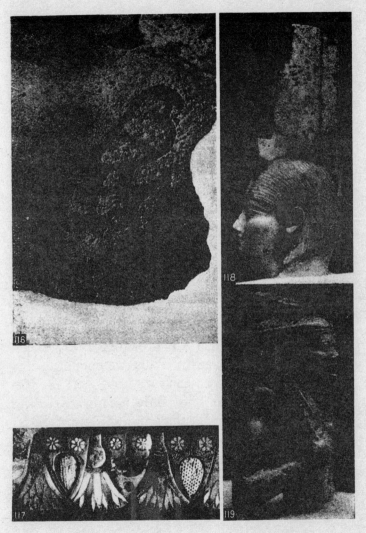

116. Two-colour glaze of Mena
117. Lotus border (XXth dynasty)

118. Head of Isis
119. Royal fan-bearer

blue-green glaze. The front is ribbed in imitation of reedwork, and they probably were copied from reed mats used to line the walls. Part of a tile has large hieroglyphs inlaid in colour, showing that decorative inscriptions were set up. Rather later, at the beginning of the IIIrd dynasty, there is the doorway of glazed tiles of King Zeser, with his name and titles in various colours; this doorway, now in Berlin, belonged to a room in the Step pyramid entirely lined with glazed tile.

Smaller objects were also made in glaze. A tablet of the first dynasty bears a relief of the figure and titles of an aboriginal chief, apparently made to be left as a memorial of his visit to temples—a sort of visiting card,—as it was found in the temple of Abydos. Figures of women and animals were found with it, and glazed toggles to be used in place of buttons on garments. Very little glazing has been preserved to us from the pyramid age; there are small tablets with the name of King Pepy (4100 B.C.) in relief, but roughly done.

The general colour of the early glaze is greenish-blue or blue-green, never distinctly of either colour. Such appears from the prehistoric age to the pyramid time. The glaze is full, and was not heated long enough to soak into the body. It often has pit-holes in it, and does not seem to have been very fluid. In the VIth dynasty a second colour appears, a dark indigo blue; this is on a scarab of Merenra, and on small toilet vases of the period. Some earlier scarabs are probably of the age of the IVth, and even of the IIIrd dynasty; these have a clear brilliant blue glaze, thin and well fused.

In the XIIth dynasty the glaze is thin and hard. On ring-stands and vases it is often dry and of a greyish green. A rich clear blue glaze was also used, and is best seen on scarabs and on the favourite figures of hippopotami, which were only made in this period. The designs and inscriptions in the glaze were of a fine black, apparently coloured with manganese.

The XVIIIth dynasty was the great age of the development of glazing. It began with so close a continuance of the style of the XIIth dynasty that it is hard to discriminate one from the other. Down to the time of Tahutmes III the small pieces and beads with blue colour are as those of the previous age; but the large bowls are of a brighter blue and rather a wetter glaze. At the beginning of the dynasty there is also a dark green glaze used upon schist, mostly seen on the elaborately carved kohl pots. Under Amenhotep II was made the largest piece of glazing that is known from Egypt, now in South Kensington Museum. This was a great *uas* sceptre made as an offering, the stem of which is five feet long. This length was built up of separate sections of body ware, made each about nine inches long, so as to have sufficient firmness ; after they were each baked they were then united with a slip paste of the same ware, and finally fired with a single flow of glaze over the whole five-feet length. The head was made separately. The special difficulty of firing such large pieces is to maintain a uniform heat over the whole, and to avoid any reducing flame from the fuel, which would discolour the glaze, and produce lustre ware. The heating must also be brief, so as to avoid the glaze running down, or soaking into the porous body and leaving it dry.

Under Amenhotep III and IV the art of glazing reached its most brilliant development, both in its colours and in the variety of its applications. Beside the previously used shades of blue and green we meet with purple-blue, violet, a brilliant apple-green, bright chrome-yellow, lemon-yellow, crimson-red, brown-red, and milk-white. Besides the previous uses of glaze for bowls and vases, beads and scarabs, we now meet with a great variety of pendants and ornaments for necklaces, more than two hundred and fifty forms of which are known from the objects and the moulds ; also flat emblems and name plaques, with stitch holes or loops at the edge, for stitching on to the muslin dresses then worn. The private person thus wore the king's name on his arm, and the king wore the titles of the sun-god to whom he was devoted. The effect of the white muslin dresses with dazzling blue plaques and natural coloured daisies and other flowers scattered over them, must have been very striking. Another use of glaze was for architectural inlaying (fig. 117). The capitals of great columns were inlaid all over with stripes of red and blue along the palm leaf design, separated into small squares by gilt bands between. The whole capital was thus copied on a vast scale from cloison jewellery. Another use of glaze was for inlaying coloured hieroglyphs in the white limestone walls. This system was carried on in a simpler way into the next dynasty, where a great quantity of cartouches of Sety II are known ; and in the walls of the temple of Luqsor are rows of holes of corresponding size, from which they have probably been taken. A favourite form of glazed ware in the XVIIIth and

GLAZED WARE

XIXth dynasties is that of the graceful lotus flower cup.

In the XIXth dynasty there is much less variety of glazing; but we meet with the rise of a new industry which was to eclipse all the others in its output. Sety I had many glazed figures of *ushabtis* of blue colour inscribed in black, or of glazed steatite, in his tomb. Under Ramessu II they became usual for private persons, and for a thousand years later they were made in enormous numbers, usually four hundred being buried in any wealthy tomb. The Ramesside *ushabtis* are usually green with black inscriptions, rarely white with purple. In the XXIst dynasty they are of very intense blue with purple-black inscriptions, and very roughly made, deteriorating throughout the dynasty. In the XXIInd and XXIIIrd dynasties they are small, and usually green and black. In the XXVth they are mere red pottery dipped in blue wash, or little slips of mud were substituted. The XXVIth dynasty started a different class of very large figures, up to ten inches high, beautifully modelled, with incised inscriptions, back pillar, and beard, always of green glaze; and these deteriorated to Ptolemaic times, excepting that there are some splendid blue ones of Nectanebo, and smaller ones of bright colour with ink inscriptions of private persons of his time.

About the XXVIth dynasty, glazed figures of the gods were made for popular use, and by about 300 B.C. they appear in vast numbers, very roughly moulded. Some of the earlier pieces are very beautifully modelled, and glazed so exactly that the hollows are not at all filled up. A head of Isis (fig. 118), and a half-length figure of a fan-bearer (fig. 119) are perhaps the finest pieces of such work. The latter figure is remarkable for the vigour of the muscles and the overbearing official dignity of the expression.

Great numbers of amulets were also made to be buried with the mummies or worn by the living. The earlier examples are fairly modelled, of apple-green tint; in Persian times they are sharp and dry in form and of an olive-grey colour, but they became very roughly and coarsely moulded in Ptolemaic times. There are some interesting modelled heads of this age, covered with blue or green glaze, such as a Ptolemaic queen, and a woman wearing a face veil. Vases of Greek and Roman styles were also common. A delicate thin ware with Assyrian-esque figures, in white on a slightly sunk blue ground, was made in the Persian time and continued into the Ptolemaic age. Large blocks for legs of furniture, and stands, were also made now. The characteristic colours are of a dark Prussian blue bordering on violet, and an apple-green.

In the Roman age there is an entirely new style. The body of the vase is of a purple-black colour, with a wreath of bright green leaves around it. Such continued almost to Coptic times. The bulk of the Roman glaze is of coarse forms, and bright Prussian blue in tint. The vases have animals in relief, apparently under Persian influence. The flat trays with straight sides are copies of the silver dishes of the time. The old style of glazing con- tinued down to Arab times; a steatite amulet, in the cutting, and colour of the glaze, might well have been of the Shishak age, but for the Arabic inscrip- tion upon it. And at the present day some credit- able imitations of ancient glazing are made for fraudulent trade at Thebes.

Turning to the more technical matters, the body of the ware is always a porous, friable, siliceous paste; in some cases so soft that it can be rubbed away from the broken surfaces by the finger. The unglazed beads and figures occasionally found can hardly be handled without breaking. This paste was moulded roughly into form, and when dry it was graved with a point to give the detail. If it broke in the fingers a good figure would be stuck together again with a scrap of the paste before glazing. Large objects were made in sections, dried and baked, and then joined up with some of the same paste, and re-baked before covering with glaze. In the XXVIth dynasty there is a beautiful hard stoneware, apparently made by mixing some glaze with the body, enough to fuse it together into a solid mass throughout. The surface of these works is always very fine and smooth, without any face glaze, but only the compact polished body. The usual colour is apple-green, but violet is sometimes found in the early examples of the XVIIIth dynasty.

The colours were rarely anything beyond shades of green and blue. These were produced by compounds of copper; the blue is especially free from iron, which even in traces produces a green tint. The blue if exposed to damp fades white; the green changes to brown, owing to the decomposition of green silicate of iron and the production of brown oxide of iron. This decomposition may go on beneath an unbroken polished face of glaze, changing the glaze to brown. The shades of blue and green were all experimentally produced in modern times by Dr Russell, F.R.S., who succeeded in exactly copying the purple blue, full blue, light blue and French blue, and the green-blues and full greens in more than a hundred tints. The method was indicated by the half-baked pans of colour found at Tell-el-Amarna. Quartz rock pebbles had been collected, and served for the floor of the glazing furnaces. After many heatings which cracked them they were pounded into fine chips. These were mixed with lime and potash and some carbonate of copper. The mixture was roasted in pans, and the exact shade depended on the degree of roasting. The mass was half fused and became pasty; it was then kneaded and toasted gradually, sampling the colour until the exact tint was reached. A porous mass of frit of uniform colour results. This was then ground up in water, and made into a blue or green paint, which was either used with a flux to glaze objects in a furnace, or was used with gum or white of egg as a wet paint for frescoes.

The ovens were small, about two or three feet across; cylindrical pots were set upside down and a fire lighted between them, and the pans of colour rested on the bottom edges of the pots. In Roman times the glazing furnaces were about eight feet square and deep, with an open arch to windward half way up. The vases and dishes were stacked in the furnace upon cylinder pots, and the successive dishes in the piles were kept apart by cones of pottery nearly an inch high. The failure of a furnace-load has revealed the system; by too long heating the glaze soaked through the porous body, and it all settled down and partly fell to pieces.

The other colours used were: for the red a body mixed with haematite and covered with a transparent glaze; bright yellow, the composition of which is unknown; violet in various depths, from a faint tinge on the white lotus petals to a deep strong colour, probably made by copper blue and one of the purples; purple in various strengths from a rich bright tint upon white to a black purple for designs upon blue, all produced by manganese; occasionally purple-blue made with cobalt; dead white, which was doubtless produced by tin as at present.

Before leaving the subject of glazing we may notice the system of moulding pendants and figures in red pottery moulds, of all sizes from a quarter of an inch to three or four inches across. A great variety of these is found at Tell-el-Amarna of the XVIIIth dynasty, and at Memphis of later periods. They sometimes contain the remains of the siliceous paste with which they were choked when they were thrown away. At Naukratis hundreds were found for making scarabs for the Greek trade. The moulded objects were covered with glazing wash, and put into the furnace. Beads were commonly made on a thread, dried, and the thread burnt out; they were then dipped in glaze-wash, and fired. In early times small beads were rolled between the thumb and finger on the thread, producing a long tapering form like a grain of corn.

There has been much misunderstanding about the age of glass in Egypt. Figures of smiths blowing a fire with reeds tipped with clay have been quoted as figures blowing glass, though no blown glass is known in Egypt before Roman times. A cylinder of glass of King Pepy has been quoted; but this is really of clear iceland-spar or selenite lined with coloured paste. A panther's head with the name of Antef V has been called glass, but it is really of blue paste. Various pieces of inlaid stone jewellery have been mistaken for glass, but none such is known till late times.

There does not seem to have been any working of glassy material by itself, apart from a base of

stone or pottery, until after 1600 B.C. The earliest
dated pieces are an eye of blue glass imitating turquoise, with the name of Amenhotep I (1550 B.C.),
and a piece of a glass vase with an inlaid name of
Tahutmes III. Beads of this age are plain black
with a white spot on opposite sides; black and white
glass cups probably belong to the same date. The
variety of colours quickly increased, and by the time
of Amenhotep III and IV, about 1400 B.C., there
were violet, deep Prussian blue, light blue, green,
yellow, orange, red (rare), clear white, milky white,
and black.

The designs were entirely ruled by the method
of manufacture. The glass was never cast, but was
worked as a pasty mass, and all the decoration was
made by inlaying threads of glass drawn out to
various thicknesses. The actual production of the
glass we deal with below. The patterns on a vase
or bead were produced by winding threads around
the body, and then dragging the surface at regular
intervals (figs. 120, 121). If dragged always in one
direction, it made a series of loops or U pattern; if
dragged alternately each way it made an ogee pattern. Around the neck and foot a thick thread was
often put on, with a thin thread spirally round it,
usually white with black spiral. The forms of the

120, 121. Vases (XVIIIth dynasty)   122. Mosaic (late)

GLASS

vases are those usual in other materials at this period,
such as ⬭⬯⬮. This same method was fol-
lowed in the glass found at Cumae near
Naples, dating from about 700 B.C. It is distinguished from the Egyptian fabric by a duller surface and duller colouring, and a common form unknown before is ⬭. This later glass is usually
mixed with the earlier in museums, and occasionally it is difficult to distinguish it ; but both the
forms and the colour leave very little doubt as to
the age.

This system of winding threads of glass was
usual for beads also. A mere chip of a glass bead
can be distinguished, whether Egyptian or Roman,
by the direction of the streaks and bubbles in it.
The early glass is all wound, with lines running
around ; the Roman glass is all drawn out and
nicked off, with lines running along ; the medieval
and modern Venetian beads are again wound, and
some of the recent ones closely imitate Egyptian
dragged patterns, but can be distinguished by the
opacity of most of the colours.

The XVIIIth dynasty workers also cut and engraved glass, though but rarely. They sometimes
produced a clear glass entirely free of colouring, even
in a thickness of half an inch. About the XXIIIrd

dynasty (750 B.C.) a clear, greenish Prussian blue glass was usual for beads, and continued to Persian times for scarabs (500 B.C.). Rather later, about 400–200 B.C., there appears a large development of opaque glass figures of hieroglyphs, cut and polished, to inlay in wooden caskets and coffins. Opaque red and blue to imitate jasper and lazuli were the most usual colours. Figures of the four genii of the dead and other usual amulets were commonly made by pressing the glass into moulds while heated. A favourite colouring for such was a deep, clear, true blue, backed with opaque white to show up the colour.

About the later Ptolemaic time and through the Roman age the main work in glass is that of minute mosaics (fig. 122). They were built up with glass rods, heated until they half fused together, and then drawn out so as to produce a great length of much reduced section. Thus patterns of extreme delicacy were produced; and one single piece of construction could be cut across into a hundred slices, each repeating the whole design. The patterns are sometimes purely Egyptian, as *ankh* and *uas* alternately, but more usually Roman, such as heads and flower patterns. Such mosaics were mounted in jewellery, or, on a coarser scale, set in large designs for caskets and temple furniture.

GLASS

The characteristic of Roman times is the use of blown glass. The cups, bottles, and vases were nearly all blown, often with threads woven around, dabs attached and impressed, or patterns stamped while soft. The feet of cups were modelled into form while pasty, the tool marks showing plainly upon them. Ornamental stamps were pressed on soft lumps put on the sides of vases. Such stamps became used for official marks, and in early Arab times they registered the substance for which the glass measure was intended, also the amount of the capacity, and the maker's name in many cases. Another main development of Byzantine and Arab glass was for weights, usually to test gold and silver coins, but also for larger amounts up to a pound. These weights bear the stamps of the Byzantine epochs in a few cases, but are found by the hundred of the VIIIth to Xth centuries, and by the thousand of the Xth to XIth centuries, dying out at the early crusading age.

We now turn to the purely technical side, to describe the process of manufacture in the time of Amenhotep IV, about 1370 B.C., when it is best known to us, from the remains of the factory at Tell-el-Amarna. A clear glass could be produced, which was usually not quite colourless, but sufficiently so to take up various colours. It was free of lead and borates, and consisted of pure silica from crushed quartz pebbles, and alkali doubtless from wood ashes. It was fused in pans of earthenware. This glass was coloured by dissolving the blue or green frit in it, or mixing other opaque colours. Samples were taken out by pincers to test the colour at different stages. The whole mass was fairly fused, and then left to get cold in the earthen pan, which was about four or five inches across, and held half an inch to an inch deep of the glass. When cold the pan was chipped away, the frothy top of the glass was chipped off, and lumps of pure glass were obtained free from sediment and scum. A lump of glass thus purified was heated to a pasty state, and patted into a cylindrical form, then rolled under a bar of metal, which was run diagonally across it, until it was reduced to a rod about the size of a lead pencil, or rather less. Such a rod was then heated, and drawn out into "cane" about $\frac{1}{8}$ inch thick. Every vase was built up from such cane.

For making a vase a copper mandril was taken, slightly tapering, of the size of the interior of the neck. Upon the end of this was built a body of soft siliceous paste, tied up in rag, and baked upon it, of the size of the interior of the intended vase.

GLASS

The marks of the string and cloth can still be seen inside the vases. On this body of powdery material glass cane was wound hot until it was uniformly coated. It was re-heated by sticking the end of the mandril into the oven as often as needful; glass threads of various colours were wound round it; and the whole was rolled to and fro so as to bed in the threads and make a smooth surface. A brim, a foot, and handles were attached. Finally, on cooling, the copper mandril contracted, and could be taken out of the neck, the soft paste could be rubbed out of the interior, and the vase was finished. The final face is always a fused surface, and was never ground or polished.

A similar mode was followed for the glass beads. The thread of glass was wound upon a hot copper wire of the size of the hole required; and after piling on enough, and completing the pattern of colour the wire contracted in cooling and could be withdrawn. The little point where the thread of glass broke off can be seen at each end of the beads.

CHAPTER XI

THE POTTERY

THE varieties of pottery are so extensive that from the prehistoric age alone a thousand are figured, and the later ages give at least thrice that number. We cannot attempt to give even an outline of a subject which alone would far outrun this volume. A single most typical form of each main period is here shown, to illustrate the entirely different ideas which prevailed.

Forms.—In the prehistoric age many of the forms have no marked brim. The bowls, conical cups, and jars simply end at a plain edge, like this marked Pre. Brims were more usual in the later prehistoric age. A great variety of fancy forms appeared—double vases, square bottles, fish, birds, or women were modelled; and as the whole pottery was handmade, such were no more difficult to make than circular forms. On coming to the Ist dynasty the forms were

126

more clumsy, such as that marked I; and some of
the earlier forms were continued in a very degraded
state. The main feature is the class of very large
jars, two to three feet high, which were used for stor-
ing food and drink. This class rapidly deteriorated

PRE·   I   V   XII

XVIII   XIX   XXVI   RO·

and became almost extinct by the IIIrd dynasty.
In the pyramid age some neatly-made pottery is
found; thin sharp-brimmed bowls were usual, and
the form marked V, with a sharply pointed base,
was peculiar to this time. By the XIIth dynasty the
globular or drop-shaped pot was the prevalent type,
and varies in size from a couple of inches to a couple

of feet. Drinking-cups of a hemispherical form, very thin, without any brim, are also of this age. The XVIIIth dynasty was begun with long graceful forms, such as XVIII ; and later some beautiful long-necked vases are found. All of these forms rapidly degraded in the XIXth dynasty, and ugly small handles come into use, probably influenced by Greek design. In the XXVIth dynasty, lids with knob handles became common, and accordingly the brim disappeared, and a plain edge was used which could be easily capped. The large jars of this age are of Greek origin. During the Ptolemaic time debasement went on ; and the most ugly, smug, commonplace forms belong to the Roman age. They are mostly ribbed, as in this marked Ro. The big amphorae begin with ribbing in the latter part of the second century, in broad fluting curves. These became narrower and sharper, until in the sixth and seventh centuries the ribbing had become almost a mere combed pattern around the jar. The jars also decreased in size, were thicker, softer, and coarser, until the type vanished with the Arab times.

Decoration.—The earliest painting on prehistoric vases was of white slip, in line patterns, copied from basket-work, and rarely in figures, such as fig. 65.

THE POTTERY

This white paint was put over a bright red facing of haematite ; and such red and white pottery is still made with closely similar patterns by the mountain tribes of Algeria, where the style seems never to have died out. The black tops of the early red vases we shall deal with under Materials. The later pre-historic painting was in dull red on a buff body, such as fig. 66. In the pyramid age there was only a polished red haematite facing, and in the XIIth dynasty even this was not used. About the XVIIth dynasty a fine red polish was common, which ceased early in the XVIIIth dynasty ; white on the brims, or dabbed in finger-spots over the inside of saucers, was also of the XVIIth dynasty. Black or red edges to pottery next appeared, and by Tahutmes III there was a style of narrow black and red stripes alternating. The use of blue paint, of copper frit, began under Amenhotep II, but it was not usual until Amenhotep III, and it was common until the close of the XIXth dynasty, though much flatter and poorer than at first. After this there was no decoration on pottery until the late Roman time. About the age of Constantine a hard, fine pottery came into use, with a thin red wash on it, and often of a pale salmon colour throughout. When the southern tribes pushed down into Egypt, the brown and red patterns which were usual in Nubia were carried with the invaders, and such painting was the main influence in the painted Coptic pottery.

Materials.—The prehistoric pottery of the earlier period is all of a soft body, faced with red haematite. As the pots were usually baked mouth downward, the brim was covered with the ashes; and these not being burnt through, reduced the red peroxide of iron to the black magnetic sesqui-oxide, such as is familiar to us in the black scale on sheet steel. The interior of the pots is likewise black, owing to the reducing gases from the ashes below; rarely the heat after the combustion has lasted long enough for the oxygen to pass through the pottery, and so redden the inside. Open dishes were also haematite-faced inside, and the iron is reduced to a brilliant mirror-like coat of black all over. The reason of the polish being smoother on the black than on the red parts is that carbonyl gas—which is the result of imperfect combustion—is a solvent of magnetic oxide of iron, and so dissolves and re-composes the surface facing. On once understanding the chemistry of this, it is needless to discuss the old idea that smoke blackened this pottery. Smoke—or fine carbon dust—could not possibly penetrate through close-grained pottery, and the black extends all through the mass, naturally owing to the action of reducing gases to which the pottery is quite pervious. There may perhaps be some other kinds of black pottery influenced by smoke ; but it is far more probable that all black pottery is due to black oxide of iron produced by imperfect combustion, which is accompanied by smoke.

In the later prehistoric age the pottery has a hard reddish buff body with white specks. In the pyramid period a smooth soft brown body is usual. Hard drab pottery also appears in the Vth and VIth dynasties. In the XIIth dynasty the common soft brown body is general, and extends to the XVIIIth. By the middle of the XVIIIth dynasty a hard drab ware with white specks and faced with a drab polish is very characteristic, and continues into the XIXth. Thence onward the brown body reasserts itself, with some inferior greenish drab ware about the XXIInd dynasty. Greek clays appear during the XXVIth, but probably all imported from Greece. Soft red pottery belongs to the Ptolemaic age. But the old soft brown rules in the Roman time, being at its worst in the early Coptic. The thin hard ware of the Constantine age is apparently not native, and may be due either to Nubian or Roman influence.

Modelling.—A constant use of pottery for modelling should be mentioned, although we cannot illustrate such a large subject here, as it is only subsidiary to stone-work in each age. In the prehistoric time rude figures are often found, both of men and women. Little is known of pottery modelling in the Old and Middle Kingdoms. Rough figures of cows are placed upon the brims of bowls about the XIth and XIIth dynasties. In the XVIIIth–XXVth dynasties a large use of roughly modelled *ushabti* figures of servants prevailed. But it is rarely that the other modelling is apart from foreign influence. A class of exquisitely formed figure-bottles, of women and animals, was made of fine foreign clay, probably by Greeks, at this age. Also rude solid figures of men and horses extend from this time onwards. The great age of pottery figures begins with the modelled heads of foreigners from the foreign quarter of Memphis, certainly due to Greek admixture. These are admirably done, and each hand-modelled singly. They begin about 500 B.C., and by about 300 B.C. moulded figures come into use. At first these are solid, but from about 200 B.C. down to 300 A.D. they are moulded hollow, being made of a front and back half united. The enormous number of these figures, and of figure-lamps made similarly, is very familiar

THE POTTERY

from the Roman period. It is remarkable what good work is shown in some figures even as late as 250 A.D. The late dating of the figures and the varieties of the lamps are illustrated in *Roman Ehnasya* from my own excavations.

CHAPTER XII

IVORY-WORKING

In prehistoric times ivory was much used, doubtless owing to the elephant being still abundant in southern Egypt. The natural form of the tusk was often left, and the surface worked in low relief; but the earlier work was on small pieces, as in figs. 3, 15, 17. Not only elephant ivory was used, but also that of the hippopotamus. At the beginning of the Ist dynasty ivory was largely used for statuettes and carvings. One of the best examples of this school is the figure of the aged king (fig. 21). Many other carvings of girls, boys, apes, lions and dogs were found with this at Abydos. At Hierakonpolis a great mass of ivories was found in a trench six feet long, and many of them have been preserved. They are figures of men and women, carved tusks, wands, and cylinders. In the tomb of Mena's queen at Naqadeh were ivory lions and dogs, and such were also found in the tomb of King

IVORY-WORKING

Zer at Abydos, used for gaming pieces. All of this early ivory-work is vigorous, and has the character and spirit of the early art.

The finest work known in ivory is the portrait of Khufu, the builder of the great pyramid (fig. 123). It is here much magnified, as the face is only a quarter of an inch high. Yet in this minute space one of the most striking portraits has been given. The far-seeing determination, the energy and will expressed in this compass, would animate a life-size figure; indeed, it would be hard in the illustration to distinguish it from a work on a large scale. The correct position of the ear should be noted, as it is always put too high up in later sculpture. Quite apart from the marvellous minuteness of the work, we must estimate this as one of the finest character-sculptures that remain to us.

A piece of open work, of a girl standing, is probably of the Old Kingdom (fig. 124). It is not of the style of hair or treatment of the Middle or New Kingdom; and in the Saitic age, when the older style was copied, the work is worse in pose and much more detailed and punctilious. There are some beautiful pieces of architectural models in ivory, from the inlaying of a casket, and, also, a figure of the Vth dynasty.

Of the Middle Kingdom an ivory baboon is perhaps the finest work ; it has disappeared from the museum when at Bulak, and its place is unknown. A broken figure of a boy carrying a calf shows great truth and spirit. Ivory was also used for lion-head draughtsmen in the XVIIIth dynasty, but there are no fine works of that time.

Of the XXVIth dynasty two fine pieces have been found at Memphis, a lotus flower (fig. 125) and a man bearing offerings (fig. 126). These had been applied to the sides of caskets or other small woodwork. The figure of the man is but a stiff and coarse copy of the Old Kingdom work, lacking the truth and freedom of the early time.

There does not seem to have been any distinctive school of ivory-work in Egypt. The methods and nature of the objects are just what might have been done in stone or in wood at the same period. There is no sign of a special development due to the material, as there is in the Chinese ivory-carving.

123. King Khutu 124. Girl, Old Kingdom
125. Lotus (XXVIth dynasty) 126. Bearer of offerings

Chair, caskets, and bed of Amenhotep III

CHAPTER XIII

WOODWORK

WOOD was by no means so rare in early times as it is now in Egypt. Floyer has shown how much the desert has been stripped by the introduction of the tree-feeding camel. We see in the royal tombs of the Ist dynasty a large use of wood. The funeral chamber sunk in the ground was entirely built of massive beams and planks. The area of this room was 900 square feet in the largest tomb, varying down to 300 in the lesser. The framing of the floor, the supports, and the roof beams were about 10 × 7 inches in section and up to 21 feet in length. The planking of the floor still remains 2 to 2½ inches thick; and probably that of the roof was equal to it, as it had to bear about three feet of sand over it. The great scale of this timber work agrees with the "royal axe-man" being one of the high officials; before stone came into use, this title

137

was the equivalent of chief architect. Such a free use of wood shows that the elaborate framing of façades, which is represented as a usual pattern in early stone-work, was actually copied from wooden mansions, just as the Greek architecture was an elaborate copy of woodwork. At the close of the IIIrd dynasty we have a glimpse of the large use of wood for shipbuilding, when Senoferu built in one year sixty ships, and imported forty ships of cedar. The great gates of the temple enclosures and palaces must also have been massive works; the outer and inner pylon at Karnak had gates fifteen feet wide on either side, and over sixty feet high.

The wooden coffins of the Old Kingdom are heavy boxes with sides two to three inches thick. They are fastened together by bolts of wood; and such wooden pegs are run diagonally in different directions so as to prevent the parts being separated. Coffins hollowed out of a single block, to fit the outline of the mummy, were also used in all the earlier periods. In late times such forms were built up of boards.

For securing the joints of furniture from racking, two correct systems were used. For chairs, angle-pieces were cut from wood with bent grain, and

WOODWORK

fitted on inside the angles. There must have been a constant demand for such bent pieces, and probably they were grown into shape. In other cases forms of wood have been found which had clearly been grown for many years into the shape required. The angle-pieces can be seen under the front of the seat in fig. 128. Another system for stands was to put in diagonal bars, as in fig. 130. Sometimes merely the stiffness of deep panelling was trusted, as in fig. 129. For the backs of chairs an excellent triangular stay was made, as in fig. 127.

The light and skilful forms of the woodwork are well shown in the furniture (figs. 127–131) from the tomb of Yuaa and Thuiu, the parents of Queen Thyi, in the XVIIIth dynasty. The reliefs on the chair are carved in wood and gilded. The decoration on the casket (fig. 129) is of blue glazed hieroglyphs and inlays.

Wood was also much used for statuettes. The ebony negress and other figures (figs. 40–42) show it on a small scale; larger figures were also made, such as several in the Turin Museum, and some of life-size, but the latter are coarser in work, as the figure of Sety I in the British Museum. A fine figure almost life-size remains from the XIIIth dynasty, King Hor, in the Cairo Museum.

A system of inlaying coloured stones, glazes or glass, in wood as a basis, is found as early as the Vth dynasty, in the model vases of Nofer-ar-ka-ra. In the XVIIIth dynasty this method of decoration is seen on the gigantic mummy-cases of the Queens Aah-hotep and Aahmes, which were inlaid, probably with lazuli. The inlay was so valuable that soon after it was all prised out with the corner of an adze, and blue paint substituted for it. In the XXIIIrd dynasty decorative figures were wrought in wood, with the whole detail in inlay, as in the group of Pedubast. And in the Greek period large wooden coffins were encrusted with inlay of coloured glass, and the sides of wooden shrines were similarly the basis for brilliant polychrome adornment.

Regarding the methods of woodworking, certainly the axe was the primitive tool, as shown by the royal architect being designated by the axe. In the scenes of the pyramid age we find the saw about three feet long worked with both hands, the mallet and chisel for cutting mortise-holes, and the adze in constant use for shaping and for smoothing wood. To this day the small adze is a favourite tool of the Egyptian carpenter and boat-builder. For smoothing down the caulking inside a boat, heavy pounders of stone were used, held by a handle worked out on each side of the block. Drills were also commonly used both on wood and stone, worked by a bow. The subject of tools and their variations is a very wide one, which cannot be entered upon here.

CHAPTER XIV

PLASTER AND STUCCO

In the masonry of the pyramids plaster is constantly used, both to fill joints as a bedding, and to level up hollows in a face. The plaster used is a mixture of ordinary lime and plaster of Paris, the carbonate and sulphate of lime. How it was introduced into the joints of the pyramid casing is a mystery. The blocks at the base weigh sixteen tons, so that no free sliding to reduce the joint-filling could be done; yet the vertical joint, five feet high and seven feet long, is filled with a film of plaster only a fiftieth of an inch thick. The joints of the masonry in the passages and chambers are all filled with plaster, though so close as to be almost imperceptible. In the core masonry a coarse plaster was poured between the stones and filled into hollows. The flaws and defects in the faces of stones were freely filled with plaster, which was coloured to match the stone. In rock tombs plaster was used to fill up cracks and hollows ; and it often remains in perfect condition while the rock around has decayed.

Plaster was also used on the brick walls, which were faced with a hard coat about a tenth to a sixteenth of an inch thick, upon which paintings were executed. By the XVIIIth dynasty this became a mere whitewash over the mud-facing of the wall. In the roughly-hewn rock tombs of that age at Thebes, the jagged surfaces were smoothed by a coat of plaster, often two or three inches thick in the hollows. A strange use of stucco was for a thin coat over sculpture, as a basis for colouring. Such a coat was even laid over statuary. In all ages this hid to some extent the full detail of the sculptor's work in reliefs. In the XIIth dynasty the finest lines were hidden by it; and on coming down to the Ptolemaic times the plasterer ignored all the sculpture below, filling the figures with a smooth daub of plaster on which the painter drew what he liked. It seems strange why the sculptors should have continued to put fine work and detail on to a surface where they were going to be at once ignored. It suggests a rigid bureaucracy in which the sculpture had to be passed by one man, and the painting by another, without any collaboration.

Stucco was used for independent modelling, as in Italy. It was laid on a flat canvas base, stretched over wood, and the whole relief was in the stucco. The chariot of Tahutmes IV is one of the main examples of such work, of which a small portion is shown in fig. 132. The relief is low and smooth, and full of detail; there is none of the sketchy rough tooling, as seen in Roman stucco reliefs. Minute details of dress and hair are all tooled in, and supply some of the best studies of Syrian robes. The varying patterns on the shields of different branches of Syrians, the feathering of the arrows, the shape of the daggers, and the flowers of the papyrus and lotus of north and south, are all most precisely rendered. It would be hard to find any point in which more details could be introduced.

Plaster was also used for casting in moulds, and for making moulds. The death mask of Akhenaten shows how such castings were produced in the XVIIIth dynasty, from a single mould without any undercutting, to serve the purpose of the sculptor as a model. Of later examples of such castings we have here a lion's head and a king's head (figs. 133, 134). They were probably made to be supplied as school copies to the workshops where the sculptors were trained. Plaster moulds are very common at

132. Stucco relief modelling (XVIIIth dynasty)
133, 134. Plaster castings for studies

PLASTER AND STUCCO

Memphis, and it is said they were even used for casting bronze work. This is very doubtful, as plaster is reduced to powder at 260° C., while moulds for bronze casting must be heated to 1500° to 1800° C.; they are more probably for casting pewter. Plaster moulds were also used for moulding pottery lamps. The oiling of plaster was done on painted plaster statuettes, so as to make them waterproof. They can still be scrubbed in water without disturbing the colour.

The most artistic use of plaster was for the modelled heads, which were placed on mummy cases in Roman times. Though most such works were rather crude, some are found which show real ability of portraiture. In fig. 135 we have a sympathetic study of the face of a young man. The lips are beautifully true, the modelling of the cheek is quite natural, the nose and brow well formed ; only the eyes have been left blank, and marked afterwards with colour. The head, fig. 136, is evidently a careful study, giving the cautious, cold expression of the man. Another face (fig. 137) is subtle, and full of feeling : the faint smile on the lips, the gracious contour of the cheek, the wavy hair, give a memory in death of a real personality. The only jarring feature is the square brow, copied from an unfortunate convention in Greek art. The eyes are here again left blank; but they seem to have been intended to be open, by the slight ridge of the raised lid. Was there a convention of regarding the dead as incapable of seeing, though seen by memory? How far these modelled heads were portraits is answered in a curious way by fig. 138. The light outline there is that of the plaster modelling, the dark outline within it is the skull from the interior of the coffin. It will be seen how exactly they agree; there is a thin skin over the forehead, then a fleshy part to the brow. Along the bridge of the nose the model closely follows the bone; below the nose the angle of meeting of the jaws exactly agrees, leaving a uniform thickness of lips; and lastly, the fleshy fulness of the chin is seen projecting. This agreement is one which the artist could never have expected to be thus tested, and therefore gives us the more confidence in his skill.

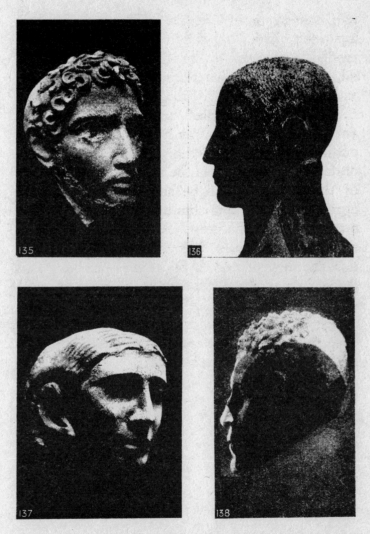

135, 136, 137. Modelled heads   138. Modelled head and skull

CHAPTER XV

CLOTHING

THOUGH leather hides, with the hair on, are found over bodies in the earliest graves, yet linen cloth was introduced early in the prehistoric times, and is frequently found wrapped around the bodies.

On reaching the first dynasty the weaving is seen to be very fine and regular, though we only have some of the stuff used for mummy wrappings, from the tomb of King Zer. The threads are very uniform, and there are 160 to the inch in the warp and 120 in the woof. Modern fine cambric has 140 threads to the inch, so it was quite equalled by hand work at the beginning of Egyptian history. A group of a dozen different cloths on one mummy of the XVIIth dynasty show 138 × 40 and 128 × 56 as the finest, and 21 × 15 as the coarsest mesh. The greatest disproportion of the threads is 138 to 40, or 3½ to 1, and the least is 70 to 62, or 9 to 8 ; it is recognised as a principle of Egyptian weaving that the woof was not beaten up as closely as the lay of the warp. Unfortunately we have scarcely any cloth except mummy wrappings, and it is not to be expected that the finest work would be thus used.

The size of the looms was considerable. The cloths on the mummy just named are up to five feet wide ; and one edge has been torn off that amount, so it was originally more. The pieces are up to sixty feet long, and yet not complete. The looms were horizontal on the ground for coarse work, such as mats ; but fine work was done on a vertical loom, and from the ease of displacing threads in tapestry the warp threads were separately weighted and not fastened to a beam. Loom weights of baked clay or of limestone are common.

A few pieces of woven tapestry have been found in the tomb of Tahutmes IV, and part of one is given here full size in fig. 139. The colours used are red, blue, green, yellow, brown and grey. The coloured threads pass to and fro over the space assigned to them, thus entirely parting the warp threads from the neighbouring ones, so that a slit is left along the vertical margins of the colours. This was remedied by stitching ; but the same weakness is seen in the Roman and Coptic woven tapestries.

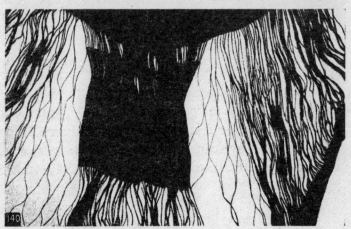

139. Coloured tapestry (XVIIIth dynasty)   140. Cut leather net

CLOTHING

These are known from the pagan period, as there are many mythological subjects; but the greater part belong to the Christian and Mohammedan ages.

The Roman and Coptic tapestries are placed upon garments as derivatives from darning, or from patches put on the garments to prevent them wearing through. The positions are broad stripes over the shoulders where any object would rest when carried, circular patches on the breasts and on the knees. On referring to the hundreds of figures in Roman dress from the third to fifth centuries (in Garucci, *Vetri ornati di figure in oro*), embroideries or tapestries are unusual in Italy. A dozen robes with scrolls or foliage patterns are shown, but only three with knee patches, and one of those (xxxi, 1) is a female servant holding an Egyptian fan, probably therefore an Egyptian slave. It seems, then, that this system of circular patches on the wearing parts is not Roman but Egyptian. Beside the woven tapestries, which are nearly all in purple, embroidery was done with the needle in white thread on the purple ground.

Leatherwork was of importance in Egypt in all ages. The two principal arts in it were the appliqué work in colours, and the cutting of network. The great example of the appliqué work is the funeral tent of Queen Isiemkheb, about 1000 B.C. It was eight feet long and seven feet wide, with sides over five feet high. Six vultures are outspread along the top, and the sides have a long inscription. The whole of the figures and signs are cut out in variously coloured leather, and stitched on to the crimson leather ground. This work we can trace in the style of earlier decorations, back to the head fillet of Nofert, fig. 24. It is also continued down to the present day in the appliqué work in coloured stuffs on the inside of Egyptian tents.

The cutting of leather nets was an art of great skill. Rows of slits were cut, breaking joint one with other, so that a piece of leather could be drawn out sideways into a wide net. One of the most delicate of such nets is partly shown in fig. 140. The square patch left in the middle of the net was for the wear of sitting on when the net was put over the linen waist cloth. Such nets over the cloth are shown in the figures of the harvesters, fig. 70, with the slit network and the square patch. To cut the leather in such extremely fine threads must have required great skill and care; and not only is the leather slit, but considerable slips have been removed so as to produce an open net close up to the edge band of solid leather; on some edges an

CLOTHING

inch or two is cut away to form one side of the
rhombic opening.

In many directions we have now traced the outlines of the artistic skill of the Egyptians, but only
outlines, which point incessantly to the wide spaces
that need to be filled in by further detail. Much of
that has yet to be discovered, but much is ready to
hand whensoever a careful observer may choose to
devote attention to any of the branches of art or
technical work which we have so briefly noticed.
In every direction a complete collecting of materials
and an adequate publication of them would bring
a full reward in results.

The powerful technical skill of Egyptian art, its
good sense of limitations, and its true feeling for
harmony and expression, will always make it of the
first importance to the countries of the West with
which it was so early and so long connected.

CHAPTER XVI

EGYPT'S PLACE IN THE ART OF THE WORLD

IN the opening chapter we have considered the point of view from which the art of Egypt—like that of every other country—must be approached. The physical conditions which surround man will necessarily control his expression of thought and his perception of beauty. Forms and designs growing out of the conditions of one land will be inappropriate in another land, and lose most, or all, of their value if transported to different surroundings. Hence it is futile to attempt to contrast the art of one country directly with that of another. We might as well compare the beauty of a tropical garden with that of an alpine forest. The only ground of comparison is that of expressing the character and emotions of the artists; and that art which conveys the mental state of the people most readily is the most perfect art. This criticism leaves aside altogether the moral question of our appreciation of the people themselves; that does not belong to art but to ethics. And before we can begin to judge of that, we must know their surroundings, and the position in which they were conditioned in the world.

Our consideration here is with the art. When we look over the varied artistic expression of different races, we see that each people has seized some one excellence, growing out of its conditions, and adapted to its feelings and utilities. We can admire each excellence in turn, and see that in each of these qualities no other people has reached the same perfection. We must recognise that artistic expression is not only shown in sculpture and painting, but in literature, mechanical design, and the amenities and adaptation of the social organism.

In Egypt, as we have noticed, the ruling principles of the art are durability, strength, and dignity, and such were the features of the national character. In vain do we look in any other country for as great an expression of any of these principles. And, with the single exception of Greece, it was also supreme in precision of work. Its work was the true expression of character, and in perfect harmony with the nature of the country.

In Crete, so far as we can yet see, the pre-eminent

facilities were the expression of motion, and the development of decorative form, and especially colour, upon pottery. Classical art never attained to the skill shown by the prehistoric art in these directions.

In Assyria, figure and animal sculpture stood very high in the best period; and the free adaptation of this to the purposes of life, as we see in the great development of friezes on the palace walls, was the distinguishing feature. No people seem to have lived amidst their art more than the Assyrians.

In classical Greece, the supremacy in vital sculpture and architectural proportion has so filled the attention of the modern world that the higher achievement of surrounding nations in other directions has been largely overlooked. In each of the special qualities that we note in other peoples the Greeks were their inferiors.

Rome was largely dominated by other races in its development; but in the art of civilisation and raising subject peoples, in the shaping of life and rule of law, it stood far above any ancient nation. In this—as in the arts elsewhere—we must look at its best period, when the impartiality and probity of its administrators brought all Greece under their sway.

The Celtic and Northern arts stood first in the

rhythm of intricate decoration, and the subtlety of the curves ; the ideal may not appeal to us, but no other region has ever produced such perfect and complex design.

In Medieval Europe, though sculpture scarcely reached the vitality of classical work, yet in expression it stood as high as in any school of art ; and in the architecture the sense of expansion and aspiration—the spiritual aspect—reaches a higher level than man has touched elsewhere.

In Italy, the expression of art in painting was its great achievement, in harmony with the character of grace seen in other lines of Italian production.

The Persian and Mesopotamian civilisation triumphed in its glorious use of coloured glaze decoration, which has been carried westward to Syria and Rhodes, and still continues in the vast domes of coloured tiles in Spain.

In Arab art we meet the exquisite calm of geometrical design with various angles, which cannot be analysed at a glance like a Roman pavement : they arrest the eye to linger over them, to seek how they arise, and what they mean.

Further east, it is difficult for us to enter sufficiently into the fundamental feelings of the races, to enable us to value their art truly. But we can at least feel the grand sense of profusion when looking at the mountainous structures of the immense topes and pagodas of India, peopled with innumerable figures on countless stages. To the minds which produce and live amongst such forms, all other work must seem poor and bare. In Chinese art we can admire the fine adaptation and the sense of minute perfection in the articles before us, the dignity and reserve shown ; and, in the literature, even a stranger to the land can feel the intimate harmony with Nature, and the mystic sense of mood in the mountains and trees and lakes around. Hardly any other poetry that we know touches the spirit of life so essentially.

The facile Japanese may well claim an unsurpassed skill and deftness in the painting of Nature, and a power to grasp the greatest amount of reality with the least means. Their perception of Nature in its strange and mysterious moods, which they show by the brush, is almost as penetrating as in the literature of China. Their exquisite sense of fitness, and of taste for beauty of workmanship, only makes us begin to realise the clumsiness of our own cast-iron performances.

To wander so far from Egypt may seem needless ; and it would be so if the essentials of other arts were more familiar in English works. We have read lately of an alleged "tyranny of the Nile"; but the real tyranny over English minds for a century past has been the "tyranny of the Hellene." The one side of art in sculpture has obscured all others; and the English mind has, with its usual idolatry, made the standard of Greece its sole measure. We need to see that a dozen national arts have each been supreme over the others in some one aspect. Then we shall see how meaningless it is to contrast the excellence of one national art with another. Each country has to confess that it has only fully expressed one aspect out of many in the immense range of human life.

Now we can begin to see the real meaning of the so-called limitations of Egyptian art. Every people has had its limitations likewise, fitting it to its conditions; and if we look at them all impartially, and not by the standard of any one of them, we shall see that the deficiencies and limitations of most races are of much the same extent. If the Egyptian had tried to render not only character, but emotion also, he would have been defying his true conditions, as much as if we put a dado of Persian glazed tiles on the Parthenon. To refer this artistic perception to the uniformity of the Nile, is about as true as if we attributed any deficiencies in German art or literature to the prevalence of cold and snow, which is a far greater tyranny than the inundation. Every physical circumstance is a factor in human work, but none of them singly dominates it. There is no point in calling the Egyptian childish in his abilities, as every other nation has been equally childish in some other respects—the Roman in his abject submission to omens, the Greek in playing with words, the Assyrian in his inaccuracy, the Arab in his drawing. In short, there is no essential difference in the capacity for showing national life and feeling by the art of each country; and in the facility and truth of expression Egypt stands in the first rank of those lands where Art has exhibited the character of man.

INDEX

Aah-hotep jewellery, 91, 92.
Aahmes I, jewellery, 92.
  II, inlaid hawk-head, 103.
Aahmes-si neit-rannu (fig. 9), 21.
Abu Simbel, 28.
Accuracy of work, 81, 82.
Ainofer servant, 16.
Akhenaten (Amenhotep IV),
  art of, 20, 53; sculpture,
  41; relief, 53; death
  mask, 144.
Alabaster sculpture, 25; vases,
  78.
Amenardys, statue of, 26, 44.
Amenemhat, III, 39, 88.
Amenhotep, I, 120.
  II, 26, 111, 129.
  III, 26, 28, 53, 111, 120, 129.
  official of, 41.
  IV, 26, 111, 120.
Amethyst beads, 80, 86.
Amulets of stone, 79.
  of glaze, 114.
Animals, real and mythical, 49.
Antef V, 119.
Antimony used, 104.
Arab art, 155.
Arch avoided externally, 6.
  known early, 64.
  form of brick, 64.
  built without centring, 65.
Architecture, 62–68.
Armlets of flint, 81. *See* Bangles.
Art belongs to country, 1, 2, 152.
  absent from copying, 2, 53.
  conditions in Egypt, 2.

Art dominated by strong light, 3.
  accepted strong contrasts, 4.
  ruled by level and vertical
    lines, 5.
  analysis by Tolstoy, 7.
  expression of character, 7–10,
    19.
  truth of Egyptian, 9.
  greatest under pyramid kings,
    16, 17.
  rapidity of development, 17,
    51.
  decay of, 18.
  of character and of emotion,
    19.
  of different peoples, 153–156.
Asiatic conquests influence art,
  19.
Assyria, art of, 154.
Aswan, school of, 27.
Axe of Aahmes, 92.

Baboon, ivory, 136.
Bak-en-khonsu, head of, 44.
Bangles, 94. *See* Bracelets,
  Armlets.
Basalt, green, sculpture in, 24,
  40.
  black, for building, 70.
Basalt, used for vases, 78.
Beads, materials of, 80.
  gold, 84.
  open-work, 94.
  glazed, 119.
  glass, 121, 125.
Bee amulet, 80.

159

INDEX

Blue, manufacture of, 117.
  paint on vases, 129.
Bracelets of Zer, 84.
  of Aah-hotep, 92.
  of Ramessu II, 93.
  silver, 93.
  gold, 95.
  Coptic, 95.
Brick building, sloping inward, 62.
Bronze, use of, 100, 101.
  origin of, 101.
Building transport, 74.
Bull hunt, 54.
Bull trampling on enemy, 14.
Bull's head amulet, 79.
Bushman type, 29.
Button seals, 86.

Canon of drawing figures, 50.
Capitals, early forms of, 67.
Captives, influence on art, 19.
Casting of gold, 85, 89.
  of bronze, 101.
  in plaster, 144.
Ceiling pattern, 58.
Celtic art, 157.
Chains, patterns of, 86, 91.
Character in art, 8, 9, 19.
Chinese art, 156.
Civil service, organizing, 16.
Claw amulet, 79.
Cleopatra Cocce (Ptolemaic), 21.
Cloison inlaying, 87–89, 93, 95.
Cobalt colour of glaze, 118.
Colossi, raising of, 77.
  weight of, 26.
Colours, making of, 117.
Columns, palm, lotus, polygonal, 67.
Comparative art, 152.
Conditions of Egyptian art, 2–5.

Conquest of Egypt by artistic race, 14.
Constantine, pottery of, 129, 131.
Contrasts of desert and cultivation, 4.
Conventions absent in early art, 15, 35, 36.
Copper, colours from, 116–118.
Copper work, 98–100.
Coptic pottery, painted, 130.
  tapestry, 148.
Copying, a degradation, 2, 17, 20, 21.
Cornice, origin of, 63.
Crete, art of, 153.
Crocodile amulet, 79.
Crowns of XIIth Dynasty, 88.
Cumaean glass, 121.

Daggers of Aahmes, 92.
Degradation of art, 17, 20, 51.
Deir el Bahri, 5, 52.
Desert, contrasts of, 4.
  art in Eastern, 25, 39.
Detail, treatment of, 18.
Diorite, sculpture in, 24, 34, 70, 78.
Divisions, political and artistic, v.
Drawing, 58–61.
Dressing stone faces, 71, 72.
Drills, tubular, 72.
  flint, 79.
Dynastic new art, 14, 30.
Dynasty I, 14, 49, 84–86, 108, 126, 135, 147.
  II, 32.
  IV, 16, 50, 129, 135.
  V, 67, 127, 131, 140.
  VI, 17, 86, 109, 131.
  XI, 17, 51.
  XII, 18, 26, 27, 36, 52, 87, 110, 127, 129, 131, 136.

INDEX

INDEX

Gold casting, 85, 89.
  wire, 85, 86, 90.
  soldering, 85, 86, 90.
  base, 94.
  over plaster, 95.
Granite, black, school of, 24.
  red, school of, 27.
  temple, 65.
  quarrying, 70, 71.
  sawn, 72.
Granulated work, 90.
Greek art, 154, 157.
  influence in Egypt, 47, 146.
  pottery figures, 132.

Hammer dressing of stone, 74.
Hand amulet, 80.
Hand work on stone vases, 78.
Harvest scenes, 56, 57.
Hatshepsut, sculpture of, 52.
Hawk amulet, 79.
  protecting king, 35.
Heads modelled in plaster, 145, 146.
Helwan quarries, 70.
Hieroglyphs, cutting of, 74.
Hor, statue of, 42, 139.
Hyaena and bull relief, 14, 49.
Hyksos type, so-called, 24, 37, 38.

Indian art, 156.
Inlaid metal, 92, 103.
Iron, rare appearances of, 104.
  sources of, 105.
  tools, 106.
  cores for bronze, 102.
Isiemkheb, tent of, 150.
Isis, head of, 114.
Italy, art of, 155.
Ivory carving, prehistoric, 12, 134.
  Ist dynasty, 31, 32, 134.

Ivory carving, IVth dynasty, 135.
  XIIth dynasty, 136.
  XXVIth dynasty, 136.

Jackal head amulet, 80.
Japanese art, 156.
Jewellery, 83–97.

Ka-aper, 33.
Kauat, princess, 51.
Keft inlaying, 103.
Kha-em-hat, tomb of, 20.
Khafra, statue of, 34.
  accuracy of, 82.
Khaker ornament, 64.
Kha-sekhem, head of, 32.
Khety, copper brazier of, 99.
Khufu, organizing by, 16.
  figure of, 34, 135.
  accuracy of, 81.
Koptos, colossi from, 30.

Lazuli beads, 80, 85.
  inlaying, 88, 91.
Lead used, 103.
Leather the earliest clothing, 147.
  appliqué work, 149.
  slit network, 150.
Lifting of stones, 75.
Light, conditions of strong, 3.
Limitations of national arts, 157.
Limestone sculpture, school of, 25.
  earliest, 31.
  working in, 69.
Linen, fineness of, 147.
Lines level and vertical in Egypt, 5.
Lion, figures of, 30, 39.
  amulet, 80.
Literature compared with art, 7, 8

INDEX

INDEX

INDEX

Statuary, late, 45–47.
  outlined and cut, 77.
Steatopygous type, 29.
Steel tools, 106.
Stone buildings copied from brick, 62.
  copied from wooden, 62.
Stone vases, 78.
Stones, moving of, 74.
Stucco on wood statues, 33, 44, 143. *See* Plaster.
  modelling, 144.
Study in limestone, earliest, 31.
Syenite used for vases, 78.
Syrian influence, 19, 66.

Taharqa, head of, 44.
Tahutmes I, 19.
  II, 40.
  III, 19, 40, 110, 120, 129.
  IV, 148, xvi, fig. 139.
Takushet inlaid statue, 103.
Tapestry, woven, 148.
  use of, on clothing, 149.
Tausert, 94.
Temple, circuit wall, 65.
  of Khafra, 65.
  of Medinet Habu, 66.
  of Dakkeh, 66.
Tin, sources of, 100.
  used, 104.
Tiryns, stone-sawing at, 73.
Toilet tray figures, 43.
Tolstoy's analysis of art, 7.
Tombs, early sculptured, 16.
  later painted, 19, 56.
Tools of modern types, 106.
Torus roll, origin of, 63.
Training of artists, 17.
Trichinopoly pattern chains, 91.
Tubular drills, 72.
Turin statue of Ramessu II, 44.

Turquoise beads, 80, 85.
Tut-ankh-amen, 42.

Ushabtis of glazed ware, 113.
  of pottery, 132.

Vases of bronze, 99, 101.
  of glass, 121, 124.
  of pottery, 127–133.
  of stone, prehistoric, 78.
    from Eastern desert.

Wall surfaces dominated by scenes, 3.
Wax used for modelling, 89, 102.
Weaving, fineness of, 147, 148.
Wigs, prehistoric, 30.
  put on over hair, 33.
Wire, 85, 86, 90.
  amulets, 90.
  plaited chains, 91.
Wooden statues stuccoed, 33, 34.
  sculpture, 42.
Woodwork, 137–141.
  early, 137.
  shipbuilding, 138.
  doors, 138.
  coffins, 138.
  furniture, 138, 139.
  statuettes, 43, 139.
  inlaid, 140.
  methods, 140.
Writing, start of, 14.

Youths' and maids' procession, 54.

Zer, bracelet of, 84.
  linen of, 147.
Zeser, glazed tiles of, 109.